Sunset KITCHENS
planning &
remodeling

SUNSET BOOKS ▪ MENLO PARK, CALIFORNIA

Sunset

SUNSET BOOKS

Vice President, General Manager: Richard A. Smeby
Vice President, Editorial Director: Bob Doyle
Production Director: Lory Day
Art Director: Vasken Guiragossian

Staff for this edition:
Developmental Editor: Jeff Beneke
Editor: Linda Hetzer
Consultant: Ed Lipinski
Art Direction: Richard J. Berenson,
　　　　　　Berenson Design & Books, Ltd.
Computer Production: Robert Steimle
Revised Illustrations: Ed Lam
Photo Research: Ede Rothaus
Assistant Editor: John Glenn
Editorial Assistants: Erica Toth, Carrie Glidden
Production Assistant: Patricia S. Williams
Cover Design: Vasken Guiragossian

KITCHENS: PLANNING & REMODELING

was produced in conjunction with Roundtable Press, Inc.
Directors: Marsha Melnick, Susan E. Meyer, Julie Merberg

First printing, eighth edition

10 9 8 7 6 5 4 3 2
Copyright © 2000, 1994, 1983, 1976, 1974,
　　　　　　1967, 1962, 1955
Sunset Publishing Corporation,
Menlo Park, CA 94025.

ISBN 0-376-01347-8
Library of Congress Catalog Card Number: 99-66306

Printed in the United States.

For additional copies of
Kitchens: Planning & Remodeling
or any other Sunset book, call 1-800-526-5111.
Or see our web site at: www.sunsetbooks.com

CREDITS

Front cover photograph by Jamie Hadley;
kitchen design by Robert Nebolon, architect.
Back cover photographs by Brian Vanden Brink (TL, TR);
Tria Giovan (BL).

Key:
T = Top; B = Bottom; L = Left; R = Right;
M = Middle; C = Center

Armstrong World Industries, Inc.: 63(BL).
Brian Vanden Brink: 3 (Thom Rouselle, Architect); 5 (TL, Korin Thomas Interior Design; TR & BR, Scholz & Barclay, Architects; BL); 6 (B, Scholz & Barclay); 8 (B); 9 & 10 (Sam Van Dam, Architect); 12 (TR, Mike Homer, Architect; B, Jane Langmuir Interior Design); 14 (T & B, Ted Wengren, Architect); 15 (B); 16 (T, John Morris, Architect; B, Sam Van Dam); 17 (Charles Allen Hill, Architect); 18(Mary Drysdale Interior Design); 19 (T, Rob Whitten, Architect); 25 (ML, Scholz & Barclay); 28 (B, Tom Catalano, Architect); 30 (Jefferson Riley, Centerbrook Architects); 31 (BL, Robert Currie Interior Design); 32 (B, Mary Drysdale); 35 (TR, Mary Drysdale; BL, Rob Whitten); 51 (T, Jefferson Riley; B); 52; 60; 62 (TL, TM, TR, BR); 63 (TL, BR); 65 (BL).
Brookhaven/Wood-Mode: 6 (T); 23 (B); 35(TL).
Phillip Ennis: 5 (C); 8 (T); 11 (TR); 12 (TL); 22 (B, Stuart Narofsky/IDT Associates); 23 (T,Vogel/Mulea); 25 (TL); 26 (B); 27 (B); 54 (KJS Interiors, Kenneth Solomon); 62 (BL).
Franke: 35 (C).
GE Appliances, GE Living Center Kitchen: 50.
GE "Profile": 57.
Tria Giovan: 22 (TL, TR); 25 (BL); 33 (TR); 36; 47 (R); 62 (BM); 65 (C, BR).
IMSI "Floor Plan 3D Design Suite": 38.
Images ® Copyright 1999 PhotoDisc, Inc.: 4 (T, B); 34 (T, B); 64 (T, B).
Kohler Co.: 56.
Kraftmaid Cabinetry: 33 (MR).
Dennis Krukowski: 47 (L, Toni Spottswood Interior Design and Space Planning).
Maytag: 58.
Merrillat Industries: 31 (TR, BR).
Moen (illustrated): 57 (BL).
Melabee M. Miller: 1 (Ellen Brounstein, Brownstone Interiors); 7 (T & B, Pat McMillan Interiors); 20 (TL, Lawrence-Mayer; TR); 21 (Steve Meltzer, Abbey's Kitchens-Baths & Interiors); 24 (Tracey Stephens Interior Design); 29 (B, Lawrence Korinda, Architects); 31 (TL); 32 (T, Rosemarie Cicio, Susan Rosenthal, Fair Haven Design); 33 (ML, Elizabeth Gillin Interiors; BL, Michael Boyette Kitchens & Baths; BR, Steve Meltzer, Abbey's Kitchens-Baths); 35 (ML); 37 (Steve Meltzer, Abbey's Kitchens-Baths); 59 (Geraldine Kaupp Interiors); 65 (TL, Tracey Stephens; TR, Lawrence-Mayor).
Multi-Pure Corp. (illustrated): 57 (BR).
Robert Perron: 5 (MR, Lyman Goff, Architects); 11 (BR, Judith Griffin Interiors/Bill Badger, Architect); 13; 15 (T, Strittmatter Kitchen & Bath); 19 (B, Judith Griffin); 20 (B, Judith Griffin); 25 (R, Elena Kalman, Architect); 26 (T, Johnson & Michalsen, Architects); 27 (T, Elena Kalman); 28 (T, David Andreozzi); 29 (T, Ronald Goodman); 33 (TL, Strittmatter Kitchen & Bath); 63 (TR).
Sub-Zero Freezer Company, Inc.: 61.
UNICLIC Glueless Laminate Flooring: 63 (TM).

A new kitchen

The kitchen is the hardest-working room in the house and probably the most complex. A successful kitchen must be well designed, efficient, and incorporate the most appropriate materials, and appliances.

A look through these pages points out the many choices available. Double sinks, professional ranges, refrigerators with through-the-door shelves, myriad choices for countertops, and a great many storage units help make the kitchen look good and function even better. This book, which includes design ideas, suggestions for efficient layouts, construction techniques, and a look at a variety of products, presents a review of the entire process from the initial planning phase through the final design to the actual remodeling.

Whether you are hiring a professional or doing the work yourself, this book will help you create a kitchen that works just right for you.

DESIGN IDEAS

For good reason the kitchen is called the heart of the home. It is where you and your family gather to cook, to eat, to socialize, and sometimes just to catch up over a quick snack or cup of coffee. Whether you're remodeling or undertaking a complete renovation of your kitchen, you'll need lots of solid information and great ideas for inspiration to make the process a success. So before you begin, study the color photographs on the following pages for design ideas you can apply to your home.

"The perfect triangle" (pages 6–11) shows how the all-important work triangle—the relationship between the sink, range, and refrigerator—can work in many different layouts to enhance a kitchen's efficiency. "Island hopping" (pages 12–15) explains how work islands—from a simple table to an elaborate storage unit with a built-in cooktop and second sink—add immeasurably to any design. And since creating a place to eat makes a kitchen a more welcoming place, "Let's eat" (pages 16–19) depicts the many ways you can pull up a chair and share a meal. "Make it hot" (pages 20–21) shows a wide selection of the major cooking appliances and their accessories, from range, cooktop, and wall oven to range hood and microwave oven.

Kitchen style comes largely from the choice of materials used for the walls, floor, countertops, and cabinets. "Surface savvy" (pages 22–25) presents a wealth of these choices and attractive ways to incorporate them in your new plan. "Seeing the light" and "Illuminating choices" (pages 26–29) offer great ideas for making natural light and light fixtures work for maximum pleasure and safety. And since no kitchen can function without lots of storage, "A new order" (pages 30–33) sets forth a range of cabinets to suit your needs.

The perfect triangle

A more accessible kitchen was the goal of this remodel. The peninsula that forms one wall of the U-shaped kitchen was set at an angle to gain more working space. A slide-in range occupies the kitchen side of the peninsula and extra counter space on the dining room side creates a serving area. The kitchen was decorated with an eye toward color and texture. The wood-trimmed white laminate cabinets and gray countertop form a backdrop for the cherry red tile backsplash and striking black range.

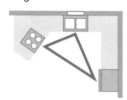

Combining function and beauty, this kitchen has a workable U-shaped floor plan with a center island and is decorated with elegant natural materials. The blond veneer that covers the flat-paneled cabinets is used on the refrigerator and the island, creating a soft contrast to the rich, dark green marble tiles covering the countertops and backsplash. Most types of marble are porous and can be eroded by the acid in substances like tomatoes, lemons, and vinegar. This marble is one of the few that can be used in the kitchen. The cooktop in the island sits between the sink and the refrigerator, creating an efficient layout. The pass-through to the dining room makes for easy serving.

A sophisticated rendition of a one-wall kitchen shows just how effective this layout can be. White enameled cabinets and a black speckled solid-surface countertop run along one long wall. Set into this wall are the prep sink and cooktop with an oven beneath it at one end (left), the main sink in the center, and a refrigerator at the other end (below). The countertop is wider at one end to accommodate the cooktop and oven and provide landing space for hot pots. There is also ample counter space on either side of the sink. Upper cabinets run along the entire wall, as do the under-the-counter cabinets. Next to the refrigerator is a floor-to-ceiling pantry, located just a few easy steps from the hall door.

The perfect triangle

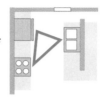

To create more space in the kitchen but still leave its basic footprint intact, part of a wall between the kitchen and an adjoining room was removed in this apartment, opening up the room and creating a small family room for eating and watching television. The appliances remain in their original positions in the kitchen space but a new countertop continues around the partial wall to form an eating counter. A section of the wall near the windows was also removed, allowing light from the kitchen window and the window of the eating area to flood the kitchen work space. The glass-fronted upper cabinets on the partial wall add to the light look. All the other cabinets—in white with white solid-surface countertops—look crisp against the warm terra-cotta tile floor.

Efficiency depends more on layout than size, as shown in this galley kitchen. The appliances are placed fairly close together in the working part of the kitchen, and the new stained pine cabinets extend all the way to the window wall on the right. There is still enough space for a small table and chairs, just right for intimate dining or a snack. The upper cabinets in this area have glass-fronted doors that make them less obtrusive next to the table. The extra counter space is the perfect spot for small appliances. The ivory walls, tile backsplash, and granite countertop are complemented by the pale sage green woodwork.

A kitchen open to the living room, dining room, and family room has to have neat, clean lines. This galley kitchen has an island that faces the family room and contains the cooktop. Directly opposite is the sink and over it is a large opening that looks out onto the hallway and living room beyond. This wall has a symmetrical look with a tall cabinet for the built-in refrigerator at one end and another tall cabinet for the wall ovens at the other end. Next to the tall cabinets are glass-fronted wall-hung cabinets for dishes and glassware. The island has a prep sink near the family room and open shelves at both ends for display and cookbooks.

The flow between a kitchen and a dining room creates synergy between the two rooms. Here the spacious L-shaped kitchen has a long island that contains the sink. The white laminate-topped countertop is surrounded by a dark wood counter several inches higher that hides any work clutter from the dining room. A stainless steel countertop along the two walls of the L unites the stainless steel appliances. The upper cabinets have frosted glass doors. The surfaces—white cabinets, glass doors, pale wood floors, and the stainless steel counter—all reflect the light coming from the large wall of windows in the dining room.

A traditional look and an efficient layout make this a hardworking kitchen. An L-shaped room with an island that contains a cooktop, the kitchen has almond recessed-panel cabinets that reflect the light from the two large windows. The main sink is under one window, a prep sink under the other. Classic touches include butcher-block countertops, wood molding, and pleated swags draped over brass curtain rods. A wrought-iron chair complements the decorative wrought-iron hinges on the cabinets.

Rustic knotty pine cabinets line this L-shaped kitchen and its L-shaped island, creating an enormous amount of storage space. The two-level island contains the cooktop, the window wall houses the sink, and the short wall holds the refrigerator—but all are close together for an efficient work space. The beige solid-surface countertops lighten the look of the dark cabinets, and the wallpaper and patterned rugs add to the country look. The island's upper level blocks the sight of food preparation from the dining room and works as a serving area.

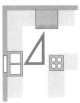

Islands divide a large kitchen into more efficient areas and add work space. Here a center island provides much-needed counter space in a large kitchen and includes ample storage underneath. The solid-surface counter is extended on one end and along one side to provide an eating area or a place to sit while preparing a meal.

A small, ceramic-tile-topped island matches the recessed-panel cabinets and the tile backsplash. It is just large enough to use as an extra counter for meal preparation, a snack, or activities like flower arranging. The side of the island facing the kitchen does double duty, providing storage for pots and shelves for cookbooks.

Kitchen islands can be movable rather than permanent installations. A long table with drawers for utensils serves the same purpose here as a built-in island: It provides a work surface and a little storage. One great advantage to a table is that it can be moved around to the spot where it's needed most—closer to the sink to help in cleaning up, by the stove to help in preparing a meal, or near the dining room, where it can serve as a sideboard for entertaining.

Big and bold, this custom-built center island is outsized in all ways, with its large marble top, its thick machine-turned legs, and its commodious storage space. The island has drawers for utensils, a shelf for large pots, cubbies for small items, and, on the side facing the cooktop, enclosed storage. The marble top can be used for meal preparation and pastry making. By its sheer size, the island in this kitchen is the focal point of the room, crowned by a striking, sunburst-style light fixture.

Islands have come a long way from a square of butcher block used as a chopping block. A long island topped with butcher block forms the outside wall of this kitchen. An integral part of the kitchen triangle, it contains the cooktop and is directly opposite the sink. On the kitchen side of the island there is storage for pots and pans. On the dining room side, shelves repeat the look of the shelves on the back kitchen wall and are used to display favorite pieces of earthenware and house a collection of cookbooks.

A well-planned island makes a kitchen efficient and fun to use. And two islands make it twice as much fun. This open kitchen is composed of one wall, which holds the refrigerator, and two islands, one that accommodates a drop-in range and another that houses a sink. Because there is only one upper cabinet, open shelving to hold glassware, the islands, and the counter next to the refrigerator do double duty as very efficient storage units. The open plan allows large windows in the dining room behind the refrigerator wall to bathe the kitchen in natural light.

One purpose of an island is to direct traffic into specific areas of the kitchen. This very long, angled island has the main sink at one end and a second prep sink at the other. It directs traffic from the back door to the dining area without passing through the working part of the kitchen, and creates a space for a small home office next to the sliding doors. The island has an undercounter refrigerator near the prep sink, making it easy for family members to get snacks and drinks without disturbing the cook.

Cooking at an island allows the cook to be part of what's going on in the room. This island is strategically placed between two pillars which, along with the oversized copper-trimmed range hood, help separate the kitchen from the dining area without blocking the view. Clad in birch beadboard panels, the island matches the kitchen cabinets. The granite countertop extends beyond the cooktop to allow guests to pull up a seat, or even to perch on a footstool, to join the cook. The six windows that surround the corner sink bring lots of light to the island.

Knowing what you want is important. This family wanted a large table for dining right in the middle of the kitchen but far away from the cooking and food preparation areas. The butcher-block table, stained to match the cherry cabinets, is attached to the kitchen work island. The matching benches are movable. The table was placed opposite the large window over the sink so there is plenty of light and a great view to enjoy during meals.

Oversized windows make this sunny kitchen the perfect spot for eating breakfast. With limited space, the island had to serve as a work surface and a dining counter, so the laminate top was extended and supported with a board that acts like a gateleg. Simple wrought-iron and wicker stools are pulled up to the counter with enough space for three to enjoy a simple meal and ample room for one to sit and pay bills, peruse cookbooks, or create a shopping list.

Integrated beautifully with the design of the kitchen, this island is made of the same wood as the cabinets and is topped with white solid surfacing that matches the kitchen countertops. Knee space was created by extending the sides of the island as well as the countertop, making the island look even bigger and more substantial. With storage on the side facing the sink, the island has room for three to eat comfortably on the other side but still has plenty of work surface for meal preparation. The woven stool seats pick up the soft green of the painted window trim.

The generous curve at the end of this large, butcher-block-topped center island provides an eating area large enough for six people or a space for guests to sit and visit. The island houses the cooktop and has ample space for meal preparation, yet space for these kitchen activities would not be compromised by family members eating a snack or doing homework, or guests catching up on the latest family news while settled on the sunny yellow stools. The island has cabinets under the cooktop for storing pots and pans and open shelving on the opposite side to display collectibles.

The wood-strip ceiling serves to define the kitchen, which is open to the hall and living room, and the support beam helps define the eating area. A countertop of laminate with wood trim is three inches lower than the island and is attached to it. Rattan-covered stools can be slipped under the counter, out of the way of foot traffic in the hallway.

By building a banquette at the dining end of this galley kitchen, there was enough room to add a large hutch for storage on the opposite wall. The long triple window brightens the dining area and makes it a pleasant place to eat. The light-colored surfaces—the white cabinets and appliances and the pale wood counters—reflect the sunlight and bring it into the working end of the kitchen.

A dramatic range hood—large enough to cover the commercial gas cooktop with four burners, a grill, and a griddle—has been integrated into the design of this kitchen. Painted the almond color of the walls and trimmed with the same tiles in shades of beige used for the countertop and backsplash, the hood coordinates with the natural pine cabinets.

A custom-made stainless steel hood sits above a black ceramic cooktop that practically disappears from view in this black solid-surface countertop. The deep curve of the hood stands in contrast to the flat cabinet doors and smooth countertop.

A slide-in electric range with a smooth cooktop has a small hood built discreetly into the cabinet above it. With the microwave oven on the shelf to the right of the range, all the cooking appliances are concentrated in one area. The white appliances blend in with the white cabinets and allow the bright blue tile backsplash to take center stage.

A cooking enthusiast has outfitted this kitchen with a six-burner, double-oven gas range and a lighted hood with a built-in shelf for spices and cooking utensils. The stainless steel backsplash unites the range and hood, making it look like one unit. The burners have space between them to allow for large pots, and the granite countertop on both sides provides plenty of landing space for hot pots.

Surface savvy

The terra-cotta floor tiles in this kitchen are set off with a rectangular border of glazed tiles in green and purple. The natural look of the tiles fits in with the etched glass panels in the cabinet doors. The soft gray of the solid-surface countertop and the warm honey tone of the cabinets allow the floor to make the color statement in this kitchen.

Bright yellow paint creates a cheerful kitchen. The cabinets were first painted a pale yellow and allowed to dry. To form the diamonds, masking tape was used to outline the diamond shapes, which were then stippled with cheesecloth in a bright yellow. The gold-toned gooseneck faucet reinforces the yellow scheme.

This polished granite countertop and backsplash look striking against the all-white cabinets and appliances. A white background makes the subtle gray and beige pattern of the granite more visible. The graphic curve of the eating counter is echoed in the curves of the chairs and the round support pedestal.

Stainless steel is durable, resistant to heat, and easy to clean, which is why it is the surface of choice in many restaurants. The stainless steel appliances, countertop, and cabinets here create a striking monochromatic kitchen that looks both substantial and luxurious. The satin finish on the stainless steel is preferable to a mirror finish, which would be too hard on the eyes.

These rich cherry cabinets have met their match in the deep blue tiles on the wall. For a totally color-coordinated kitchen, the other surfaces were chosen in one of these two colors. The countertop is solid surfacing in a blue speckled pattern, the sink is bright blue china, and the window trim is painted blue to match the tiles. Even the blinds are coordinated, with slats of cherry wood and bright blue cloth tape. The vinyl sheet flooring, in a pebbled pattern in shades of blue and rust, completes the look.

Color is a mood enhancer and the colors in this kitchen are meant to lift everyone's spirits. The bright green stain on the cabinets, which allows the beautiful wood grain to show through, and the bold blue and white tile backsplash are tempered by the long white solid-surface countertop, the white appliances, the pale yellow walls, and the light oak floors. Small splashes of red and yellow in the accessories, as seen through the glass-paned cabinet doors, add the finishing touches.

Random stripes of opaque beige and green, painted on the wood floor, are a light-hearted touch in this kitchen with its bleached pine cabinets, white solid-surface countertop, and white appliances.

A stunning backsplash of Portuguese tiles, set behind the cooktop, forms the centerpiece of this otherwise simply designed kitchen. The tiles pick up the blue of the laminate countertop and the white of the cabinets and add a bright yellow. A coordinating tile in the same three colors but with a smaller pattern forms a one-tile-high backsplash around the rest of the kitchen.

To add interest to a bank of cherry cabinets with a clear finish, glass-paned cabinet doors with a dark stain were placed over the cooktop. Long bands of the same dark-stained cherry were inset in the drawers, small squares in the cabinet doors.

Blue and white, a classic color combination that's easy to live with, always enlivens a room. Here a blue and white tile countertop and backsplash are welcoming in a room full of white surfaces. The brass faucet and towel rack and the yellow-and-white-striped bowl add spots of warm color to this already sunny kitchen.

A large picture window over the sink allows ample light into the kitchen as well as the opportunity to gaze at the beautiful view while doing the dishes. A traditional multi-paned window next to it brings light to the home office area. The white solid-surface countertop along the window wall helps reflect this light and provides enough illumination for the island work area and eating counter opposite it.

A clear glass backsplash is a surprising addition to this kitchen but it affords the cook a view of the backyard at the same time as it brings in natural light to the countertop. Most of the light in the kitchen comes from the dining area with its picture window topped by a large half-round window, its sliding glass doors, and skylight. Pendant lights reminiscent of brass lanterns provide task lighting at the peninsula.

Natural light for this kitchen
comes from the windows and door
that lead to the deck outside. To
let that light enter the dining area,
the upper cabinets over the
peninsula have double glass doors
and are filled with glassware. The
natural cherry cabinets and pale
stone countertops help reflect the
natural light and give this spacious
kitchen a warm, light-filled look.

This kitchen feels open,
airy, and full of light, but it has
just one window. To bring
light into the U-shaped area,
part of the ceiling over an old
window was removed and a
larger casement window in
a cathedral style was installed.
The pale surfaces in this
kitchen—the white-stained
cabinets, the light gray
polished granite countertop,
white appliances, glass-fronted
cabinet doors, and open
shelving—contribute to the
open, airy ambience.

Adequate light in a kitchen is an absolute must. To augment the triple window over the sink, this kitchen has recessed downlights in the cathedral ceiling for general lighting, undercabinet lights for tasks at the counter, recessed spotlights over the sink, and a multilight pendant sitting directly over the island to illuminate that work area.

Here repeating pendant lights with rounded globes complement a curved island and an arch tiled above the range hood. The fixtures provide light for tasks at the island as well as illumination for the eating counter. Small lights along the soffit of the back wall, aimed at the ceiling, radiate a soft ambient light over the entire room and can serve as night-lights for a midnight snack. Lights installed under the upper cabinets provide task lighting for work performed at those counters.

Neon lights add a dash of panache in this sophisticated kitchen. Lights over the island provide ambient light and undercabinet lights supply task lighting, so the neon tubing just sets the mood—one that's most definitely playful and full of fun.

Good kitchen lighting is functional and adds visual interest to the room. Here coordinating light fixtures enliven the room and make it a safe place to work. Recessed downlights in the ceiling provide general lighting and are helped by fixtures above the upper cabinets aimed at the ceiling. Task lighting illuminates each area where work is performed—undercabinet fixtures to light the counters, a fixture over the sink, and a lighted range hood. The track lighting fixtures add to the ambient light but can also be focused on specific areas that need more light. A light in the ceiling fan adds subtle illumination to the center island.

A new order

A separate pantry is a great asset. This one was created at the end of the kitchen and along the hall that leads to the dining room. The beautiful cherry cabinets with polished granite countertops have ample space for pots and pans and separate drawers for linens. The upper cabinets with their glass-fronted doors display china, glassware, and serving dishes. There is space for a dishwasher and a microwave oven out of the way of the main kitchen. The countertops provide a space for serving but can double as extra preparation counters when needed or as a buffet space for a party.

Upper cabinets that turn a corner were each chosen for a specific purpose. The glass-fronted cabinet displays cookbooks and glassware. The plate rack keeps everyday dishes within easy reach. And the standard cabinet holds kitchen items not meant to be on display.

White enameled cabinets line the walls of this kitchen and include a corner unit that contains an appliance garage. The center island has glass-fronted cabinets to display plates, serving dishes, and a teapot.

Built into the end wall of this kitchen is an attractive glass-fronted storage unit that shows off the owner's collections of bowls and pitchers, beside a conveniently placed wine rack for another prized collection.

To create an interesting look, this bank of cabinets includes all kinds of storage in the same bleached wood: drawers, shelves, square spice drawers, cabinets with solid doors, and ones with glass fronts.

A new order

A custom-built pantry includes slide-out shelves for food, cleaning supplies, and small appliances on the side facing the kitchen, and narrow shelves for glassware on the side facing the entry to the dining room. Storage on top of the kitchen side provides room for extra paper goods while storage above the glassware cabinet holds serving dishes and trays used for entertaining.

A butcher-block-topped kitchen island has decorative open shelves for the owner's collection of colorful earthenware bowls and plates. They sit below drawers for flatware and not so frequently used cooking utensils. The sunny yellows and golds of the crockery are echoed in other decorative accents throughout the kitchen, and the shelves offer a welcoming sight at the entrance.

Fittings for cabinet interiors greatly increase the amount of storage in a kitchen. Shown clockwise from top left: A stepped drawer organizer keeps spices visible and easy to reach; below it a drawer for pots and covers glides out for easy access. A pantry has narrow shelves that swing out to reveal more storage behind and has additional shelves on the backs of the doors. A pull-out pantry shelf unit is open from both sides to keep everything within reach. Vertical slats create storage for trays and cookie sheets. Plastic bins under the counter make recycling simple. And a lazy Susan makes good use of an awkward corner space.

PLANNING GUIDELINES

The kitchen is probably the most important room in the house and the most expensive to equip. Therefore, careful planning can help you eliminate costly remodeling mistakes while you turn your dream kitchen into a working reality. Here's how to get started.

First, you'll want to take inventory of your present kitchen. Decide what works and what doesn't and determine the extent of the remodel. Will you replace old appliances, refinish your cabinets and countertops, or move walls to create an entirely new kitchen?

Next, dream about what you want and educate yourself in the process. Start a file of photographs and information from advertisements, manufacturers' literature, decorating magazines, trade publications, and newspapers. Use the Internet to visit Web sites of manufacturers, shelter magazines, and trade groups. And visit stores and showrooms, model homes, recently remodeled kitchens, and home improvement stores to see what is available. Keep a notebook organized by subject, such as layouts and plans, color, appliances, cabinets, and so on. Based on the information you gather, make a list of everything you would like to include in your kitchen. It's a good idea to create a sample board of the materials you want in your design so you can live with the choices a while before you proceed.

Lastly, sketch your ideas on a floor plan. Then make the big decisions, but not before reviewing the costs for all your selections against your budget. Based on these preparations, and a careful review of the steps involved in the entire remodeling process as described in these pages, you should be well prepared to begin the work with confidence and to enjoy the results.

A KITCHEN INVENTORY

The success of any kitchen remodel depends on how well it suits your family—both now and in the future. The best way to get the right fit is to know not only what you want but also what you don't want. You can start by asking yourself "what is the single worst thing about my kitchen?" Then, by answering the questions below, you will have a clearer idea of what you would like and be able to assign priorities to those improvements.

Layout. The three major kitchen elements—sink, stove, and refrigerator—form what kitchen designers call the work triangle (see pages 40–41 for details). When the space allocated for these elements is right for you, the kitchen will be comfortable and efficient to work in.

- ❑ *How far do you have to walk between the sink, refrigerator, and stove?*
- ❑ *Is a wall oven conveniently located?*
- ❑ *Would a new arrangement of appliances make cooking more pleasant?*
- ❑ *How many people will be cooking?*
- ❑ *Do you have to walk through the kitchen to get to the family, dining, or laundry area? Does the path of traffic cross a leg of the triangle?*
- ❑ *How many doors open into the kitchen? Do any of them interfere with the opening of an appliance or cabinet? Do appliance and cabinet doors interfere with one another?*

Work surfaces. Lack of counter space is the bane of most kitchens and a common reason for undertaking a major renovation.

- ❑ *When you are making dinner, do mixing bowls and pots vie for counter space with a lineup of small appliances? Do dirty dinner plates have to share space with clean dessert plates?*
- ❑ *Is there a convenient work surface next to the refrigerator for unloading groceries? Next to the oven for placing hot pans?*
- ❑ *Do you need a second work surface for regular cooking?*
- ❑ *Do you want a separate surface for setting out prepared dishes for entertaining? Will this surface do double duty as a desk area? Would a pull-up or pull-out surface suffice?*
- ❑ *Is the height of the work surface comfortable or are you bending over to work? Do you need two different heights?*
- ❑ *Is the material on your countertops easy to keep clean, in addition to being the right surface for the job at hand? Do you need a heat-resistant surface near the range, a marble area for rolling out dough, or a butcher-block insert for chopping?*
- ❑ *Is there room on the countertop for items you would like to show off? And do you have extra space you can use for an appliance garage to store things you would like to keep out of sight?*

Storage. Ideally, every item in a kitchen should have its own space and be stored near where it will be used.

- ❑ *Are items you use daily such as bowls, utensils, and spices conveniently located?*
- ❑ *Is there space for pot lids, large pans, and odd-sized items? Is there space for tall items like vases or jars? Are the top shelves easy to reach?*
- ❑ *Do you have pull-out drawers in the base cabinets? Lazy susans in the corners? Do you need narrow slots for trays or cookie sheets? Do you need a wine rack?*
- ❑ *Do you have enough pantry space to store quantities of packaged food?*
- ❑ *Is the storage easy to use as well as accessible? Do the drawer runners and hinges operate smoothly? Are the handles comfortably shaped?*

Sinks and appliances. Outdated or worn appliances are one of the major reasons to remodel.

- ❑ *Is your sink large enough to hold big pans or mixing bowls?*
- ❑ *Does it have a garbage disposer?*
- ❑ *Do you want a sink with more compartments? Made of a different material?*
- ❑ *Do you need an additional sink?*
- ❑ *Does your range or cooktop have enough burners? Are they far enough apart to hold several pots at the same time?*
- ❑ *Is your oven large and well insulated?*
- ❑ *Do you want to add a microwave or convection oven?*
- ❑ *Is your refrigerator large enough for your needs? Is it noisy? Are the shelves adjustable? Are the crispers conveniently located?*
- ❑ *Is your freezer energy efficient? Would you like an icemaker?*
- ❑ *Is your dishwasher large enough for your needs? Does it get your dishes clean? Is it noisy? Expensive to operate?*

Structural changes. A completely new kitchen may require demolition and reconstruction.

- ❑ *Can windows or doors be moved? Can an interior wall be moved? Is an addition possible?*
- ❑ *Is there an attic or open ceiling above the kitchen that can be incorporated in the new design?*
- ❑ *Do you want to add a skylight? A pass-through? A second cook's area or another sink?*

Heating, cooling, ventilation. Updating these systems is important to an efficient kitchen and to healthy living and they must be incorporated into the new design at the beginning of the project.

❑ *Is the exhaust system efficient enough to rid the room of odors, grease, and heat? Can you open a window?*

❑ *Are your heating vents up to the job? Do you need to add a fan for air circulation?*

❑ *Is the air conditioning adequate?*

Lighting. A well-lit kitchen is not only more pleasant to work in but it is also safer to use.

❑ *Do you have ample natural light? Can you enlarge a window? Add a skylight? Is there a view to incorporate?*

❑ *Are counters well lit so you are not working in your own shadow? Can you see into drawers and pantries?*

❑ *Do separate areas have their own light?*

❑ *Do you have different levels of light to set different moods—well lit for food preparation, soft lighting for a late night snack, romantic for intimate dining?*

Electrical outlets. Older homes seldom have enough outlets for all the small appliances of today.

❑ *Does your kitchen have enough well-placed outlets? Are they protected by a ground fault circuit interrupter(GFCI)?*

❑ *Will you be buying more appliances in the future?*

❑ *Do you want to add an outlet strip at an appliance garage? On a center island?*

Walls and ceilings. A fresh coat of paint or new wallpaper can give new life to a kitchen. If you are changing the cabinets, walls and ceiling are likely to need work also.

❑ *What is the condition of the surfaces? Are there cracks or chips that need to be fixed?*

❑ *Is a new color scheme all you need?*

❑ *Is the ceiling too high or too low?*

Flooring. Floors take a lot of abuse so when considering kitchen changes, check the floors.

❑ *What is the condition of the flooring material? Is the floor sloping or uneven? Do you need to repair the subflooring?*

❑ *How easy is it to clean?*

❑ *Would you like a more comfortable material under foot?*

Eating area. Whether it's a large table and chairs or two stools at a counter, a space for eating makes a kitchen a more welcoming place.

❑ *How many people will eat in the kitchen? For which meals?*

❑ *Do you have space for eating that's out of the way of the work triangle? Of traffic?*

❑ *What other activities will the space be used for? Bill paying? Homework?*

❑ *If you want a table, is there enough clearance for chairs? Can a banquette be built in the space?*

Work or entertainment area. Today's kitchens often serve many uses.

❑ *Do you need a desk or alcove for paying bills, taking phone messages, or planning menus?*

❑ *Do you need shelves for a cookbook collection? A bulletin board for messages? Space for a home computer? File cabinets for family papers?*

❑ *Do you want to incorporate a television, a VCR, video games, a compact disc player, or an intercom/security system? Would you like to install a sound system?*

Special needs. If elderly or disabled people use the kitchen, you will want to consider their needs.

❑ *Is there a low counter for sitting to chop vegetables or cut out cookies? Is there a stool to pull up by the range for stirring food?*

❑ *Would a wall oven and cooktop be more convenient than a range?*

❑ *Is the sink at a convenient height?*

❑ *Are the doorways wide enough for a wheelchair? Is the eating area at the correct height? Is there sufficient room for a wheelchair to turn around?*

To Splurge or Not to Splurge?

Have you fallen in love with a vintage range or a Sub-Zero refrigerator? Would a warming drawer just complete your kitchen? Is a butler's pantry your idea of heaven? You may feel that splurging is acceptable in your dreams but not in real life. But before you dismiss any item as too extravagant, first see if it will fit into your budget and into the amount of space you have. You may choose a quality over quantity approach to your kitchen renovation, allowing yourself one great indulgence while cutting back on other items you feel aren't essential.

Developing your plan

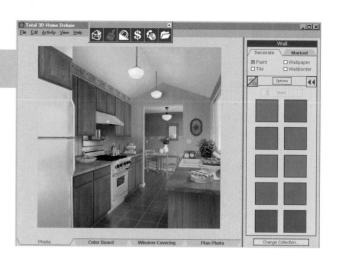

Before you begin thinking about solutions for remodeling your kitchen, it's a good idea to make a scale drawing of your existing kitchen and any adjacent areas that you may want to incorporate into a new design.

The process of measuring the kitchen elements and perimeters will increase your awareness of the existing space. Scale drawings also serve as a good foundation for future design and may satisfy your local building department's permit requirements. And if you decide to consult a professional, you'll save money by providing those measurements and drawings.

There are a number of companies that produce design software for computers that can create floor plans and elevations, straight-on views of each wall, easily and quickly using measurements from your kitchen. Computer-aided design (CAD) software shows you how a room looks in three dimensions and allows you to move walls and windows and drag appliances and other elements in and out. You can also purchase the design and layout kits that contain graph paper and appliance and cabinet templates scaled to size.

These pages show you how to measure your kitchen, record those measurements, and draw a two-dimensional floor plan to scale. You'll also learn how to measure for an elevation drawing of each kitchen wall. For more about elevation drawings, see page 45.

Tools for Measuring

You can find these items at hardware, stationery, or art supply stores.

- Retractable steel measuring tape or folding wooden rule
- Ruler or T-square
- Triangle
- Compass
- Graph paper (four squares to an inch)
- Masking tape

MEASURING YOUR KITCHEN

Measure and record the measurements accurately, since even a fraction of an inch counts in fitting together kitchen elements. Before you begin, draw a rough sketch of the kitchen perimeters (including doors, windows, recesses, and projections) and any relevant adjacent areas. Make your sketch large enough to record all the dimensions directly on it.

Measurements should be exact to ⅛ inch. It's simplest to write your first measurements in feet and inches. Don't let the tape sag while you measure. Find a partner to help you keep it taut, or use a folding wooden rule. Double-check all dimensions before you proceed.

Measuring for floor plans. A floor plan of your kitchen gives you a bird's-eye view of the layout of permanent fixtures, appliances, and furniture in the room. To make this two-dimensional drawing you'll need to measure all the walls, as well as the appliances, fixtures, and furnishings.

First, measure each wall at counter height. For example, using a hypothetical kitchen, and

BEFORE

The original floor plan shows a relatively spacious but an inefficient kitchen and breakfast area. The counter that partially separates the breakfast and kitchen areas sticks out into the middle of the traffic path from the back door to the hallway. Counter space and storage areas are practically nonexistent. Three ceiling fixtures are the only sources of artificial light in the kitchen and do not provide adequate light.

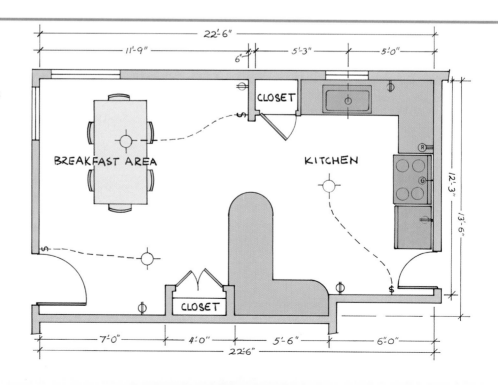

beginning at one corner, measure the distance from the corner to the outer edge of the window frame, from there to the opposite edge of the window frame, from the window frame to the cabinet, from one end of the cabinet to the other end, and from the cabinet to the corner. Note the locations of all electrical outlets and switches. After you finish measuring a wall, total all the figures; then take an overall measurement. The figures should match. If there's a difference, recheck your measurements.

Next, measure the fixtures and appliances along each wall. Note the depth and width of each appliance, the adjacent counter area, and all cabinets. If the appliance is freestanding, such as a refrigerator or range, measure the distance it extends into the room from the wall. Also note how far the doors open on all appliances. When measuring counter depth or width, be sure to include any trim, back-splash, and hardware projecting beyond the counter's edge.

Finally, make notes about the entry points of plumbing and gas lines, the direction the room's doors swing, and the depth and width of the range hood. Depending on the extent of your remodeling plans, you may also need to check the locations of load-bearing walls and partitions (see page 67). Record the dimensions of any tables, chairs, or desks that are permanent features in your kitchen.

Measuring for elevations. Elevations, or straight-on views of each wall, show the visual pattern created by all the elements against that wall. To create such drawings you'll need to know the height and width of each element. Elevation drawings of your present kitchen will look just like your room looks. Elevation drawings of your new layout will give you an idea of what the room will look like.

You've already measured the width of the fixtures, appliances, windows, and doors on each wall; now you'll need to measure the height of those elements and the height

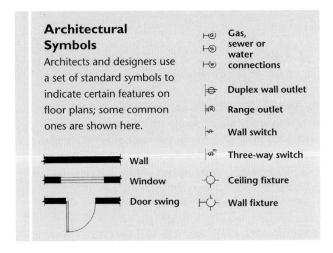

of each wall. Follow a sequence similar to the one you used in measuring a wall's length. Remember to measure the kickspace (the space between the base cabinet and floor) and the thickness of the countertops. Add all the figures and check the total against the overall floor-to-ceiling measurement. Also, note the heights of the range hood, light fixtures, window trim, and any valances.

DRAWING FLOOR PLANS TO SCALE

For neat, readable floor plans take careful measurements and be accurate converting them to scale. Kitchen designers generally use a scale of ½ or ¼ inch to 1 foot.

To begin, attach graph paper to a smooth surface or drawing board with masking tape. Use a ruler or T-square to draw horizontal lines, a triangle to draw vertical lines, and a compass for drawing the doors' direction of swing.

Complete the floor plan with your sketch as a model, using the architectural symbols shown above. To guide you, two sample floor plans, the before and after plans of the same room, are shown. The new floor plan was arrived at after many decisions were made about storage, appliances, traffic flow, lighting, and adding an office area.

AFTER

The new floor plan shows how removing the old partition and adding a large island in the center of the room greatly improves the traffic flow. The sink, now with a dishwasher next to it, and the range, which becomes a cooktop with cabinets below, remain in their original positions. The refrigerator moves to the far left side of the sink, allowing space for wall ovens and a landing area near the new cooktop. The utility sink in the island creates a second preparation area. Storage capacity increases greatly with added wall cabinets, a pantry cabinet, and a large utility closet. Recessed downlights provide lighting for the work areas as well as for an office alcove, island seating, and a dining area. A new window was added in the dining area.

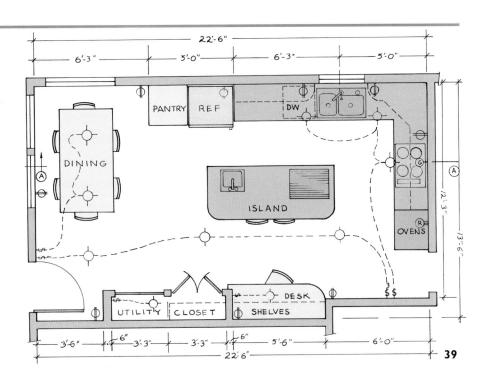

An ideal floor plan eases the cook's work and enables others to enjoy the kitchen's warmth and fragrance without getting in the way. The floor plans shown here are practical—they utilize the space well and incorporate an efficient work area—and are worth studying. For your kitchen, the dimensions of your room and your particular needs will determine the final plan.

CREATING THE WORK TRIANGLE

Ever since kitchen layout studies in the 1950s introduced the term, designers have been evaluating kitchen efficiency by means of the work triangle. The three legs of the triangle connect the refrigerator, sink, and range (or cooktop). An efficient work triangle greatly reduces the steps a cook must take during meal preparation; the ideal sum of the three legs is 26 feet or less, with no leg shorter than 4 feet or longer than 9 feet. The distance between the sink and cooktop should be the shortest leg. The work triangle should not be interrupted by the traffic flow through the kitchen.

Today, the reign of the work triangle is being challenged by two-cook layouts, elaborate island work centers, peninsulas, and specialized appliances such as modular cooktops, built-in grills, and microwave ovens. Adding a second sink also alters the traditional work triangle by taking pressure off the main work area. How much entertaining you do will help determine the location of the second sink

and which satellite appliances are grouped around it. A second sink can also alter the kitchen triangle, making it a rectangle or trapezoid. Kitchens with work areas for two cooks may have two work triangles.

New studies are under way to bring kitchen theory current with the latest designs. Nevertheless, the work triangle is still a valuable starting point for planning kitchen efficiency.

EXPERIMENTING WITH YOUR IDEAS

To experiment with new ideas for your kitchen, begin by tracing to scale the floor plan of your existing kitchen and any adjoining space you're thinking of incorporating. When space permits, don't hesitate to consider taking out walls or relocating or closing off a door or window. If the result is a more efficient and pleasant kitchen, it may be well worth the extra expense. Besides, at this stage you're simply brainstorming—you can always scale back your ideas later. If you're considering removing or relocating walls, eliminate the existing partitions in your drawing. Now try different arrangements on the tracing. As you experiment, set aside the plans that you like. Start fresh with another tracing of the kitchen's perimeter for each new layout.

Placement. In looking at the space, imagine where you'd like to perform what activities. If a window offers a pleasant view, would you rather enjoy it while eating or while washing dishes? Would you like to prepare food on an

SAMPLE LAYOUTS AND WORK TRIANGLES

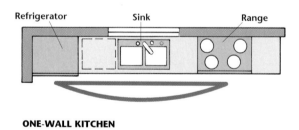

ONE-WALL KITCHEN

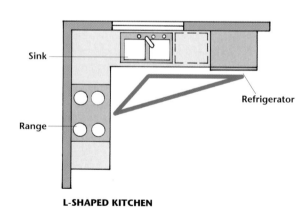

L-SHAPED KITCHEN

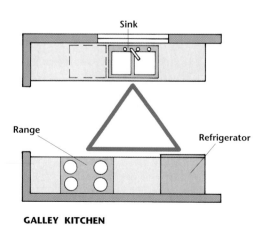

GALLEY KITCHEN

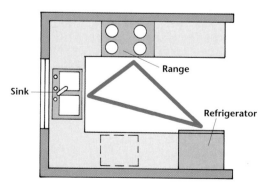

U-SHAPED KITCHEN

island or a peninsula? Imagine all the possibilities and then draw circles on the plan to represent the locations of different work areas.

Storage. Even though the details of storage and counter space will be determined later, you need to begin outlining general storage areas now. If your current plan doesn't give you enough storage space, try different configurations. Could you make room for a walk-in pantry or a wine cellar?

Layout. The layout of appliances and the lengths of work surfaces affect storage possibilities. Any space beneath counters that's not taken up by an appliance, such as a dishwasher, will be available for base cabinet or drawer storage. A garbage disposer limits storage beneath the sink; a drop-in cooktop opens up additional storage underneath.

Structural changes. Consider major or minor structural changes that would increase your options. If a window looks at a neighbor's wall, could you close it and open another wall for light and view? Would pushing out the wall a few feet allow you to add a sunny breakfast area or a baking center? Concentrate only on overall space planning for now, taking into account the traffic pattern through the kitchen at different times of day; you can work out the specifics of each work area later.

LOCATING EATING AREAS

To plan an efficient eating area in the kitchen, think first about how you'll use the space. For quick breakfasts or occasional meals, all you need is an eating counter on the outside of a peninsula or island with stools or chairs that tuck underneath. But for regular meals you'll probably want a separate table, located out of the main traffic flow.

If you don't think you'll have enough clearance for individual chairs, consider a banquette of fixed, upholstered seats or a bench. Adding a bay window can create more dining space. Also consider a table on wheels that can serve as a work surface as well as a dining table.

PLANNING SPECIAL WORK OR ENTERTAINMENT AREAS

Though a dining table or counter can double as an office and a menu-planning center, especially with storage nearby, having a space set aside for a work center is far more practical. You'll have a place to stack mail, pay bills, store cookbooks, and work—and you won't have to clean up the table when it's time to serve dinner. Plan to install a telephone here—a cordless phone is more practical than a desk phone. Also, if you plan to have a computer here, place the work area as far away from the cooking area as possible to minimize the impact of airborne grease on the computer.

If there's a gourmet cook in your family, you might want to add a specialized area for baking, barbecuing, or pasta making. Locating this cooking center away from the work triangle enables two people to work together comfortably at the same time.

If you would like music or television to accompany your cooking and dining, plan to install an entertainment center with a television, VCR, DVD, or CD player, and speakers. It's best to plan this far ahead so the proper wiring can be installed.

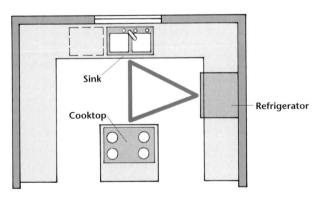

U-SHAPED KITCHEN WITH ISLAND

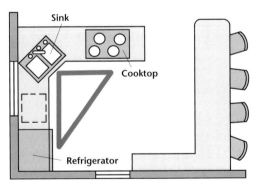

PENINSULA KITCHEN

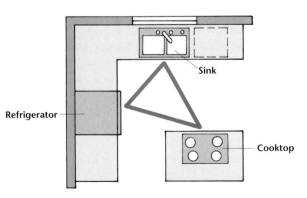

L-SHAPED KITCHEN WITH ISLAND

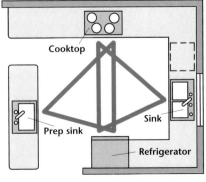

TWO-COOKS KITCHEN

The key to planning an efficient kitchen layout is to design around the four principal work centers, allowing for both adequate countertop space and storage in each area.

Listed below and illustrated here are guidelines for planning each center. Keep in mind, however, that these rules aren't absolute—in very small or oddly shaped spaces you'll need to compromise. Adjacent centers may share space, but don't count the corners, since you can't stand in front of them.

All wall cabinets should be at least 12 inches deep and 30 inches high, base cabinets at least 21 inches deep.

As a rule, items should be stored in the area of first use. The one exception? Everyday dishes and flatware: store them near the point of last use—the dishwasher or sink. As you're working out storage details, be sure to leave enough space for future purchases. If you fill every available inch with what you now have, you may soon run out of space.

REFRIGERATOR/FOOD STORAGE CENTER

Allow at least 15 inches of countertop space on the handle side of the refrigerator as a landing area for groceries. Ideally, the refrigerator is located at the end of a cabinet run, near the door to the kitchen, with that door swinging out of the room. If you need to place the refrigerator inside a cabinet run, consider a side-by-side model: their narrower doors require less clearance when open.

Make room, if possible, for an 18- or 21-inch drawer unit in this area. A smaller unit is too narrow to be useful, and 24-inch or larger drawers will almost inevitably fill up with junk.

An over-the-refrigerator cabinet is a good place to stow infrequently used items. Floor-to-ceiling open shelving or a stock pantry storage unit are perfect for the tall, narrow spot next to the refrigerator.

SINK/CLEANUP CENTER

Figure on a minimum of 24 inches of counter space on one side of the sink and 18 inches on the other. The 24-inch counter should be at the same height as the sink. For a secondary sink, allow 3 inches on one side and 18 inches on the other. It's best to locate the sink and cleanup center between or across from the refrigerator and range or cooktop. Plan for at least 60 inches of wall cabinet frontage along the sink wall.

Traditionally, designers place the dishwasher for a right-handed person to the left of the sink area and to the right for a left-handed person. Whichever position is more comfortable for you, place the dishwasher within 36 inches of one edge of the sink.

Plan to store cleaning supplies in the sink area. A large variety of bins and pull-outs—both built-ins and retrofits—are available for undersink storage. Tilt-down fronts for sponges and other supplies come on many sink base cabinets or can be installed on an existing sink cabinet.

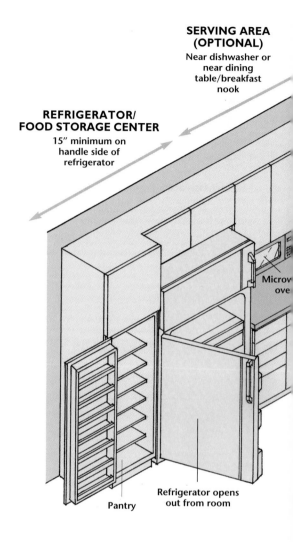

SERVING AREA (OPTIONAL)
Near dishwasher or near dining table/breakfast nook

REFRIGERATOR/ FOOD STORAGE CENTER
15" minimum on handle side of refrigerator

Microwave oven

Refrigerator opens out from room

Pantry

RANGE/COOKING CENTER

You'll need at least 9 inches of countertop area on one side and 15 inches on the other side of the range or cooktop as a landing area for hot pots and casseroles, and to allow pot handles to be turned to the side while pots are on the burners. If the cooktop is on an island or peninsula, the same rule applies. There should be at least 30 inches of clearance between the cooking surface and the surface above it. For safety sake, under no circumstances should a range or cooktop be placed under an operable window. In an enclosed kitchen, allow at least 3 inches of clearance space at an end wall protected by a flame retardant material and 15 inches of counter space on the side.

You also should allow at least 15 inches of countertop on one side of a wall oven. Typically, stacked wall ovens are placed at the end of a cabinet run; if they're in the middle, allow 15 inches on both sides. Remember that the area above the oven may get hot while the oven is on, so plan storage accordingly.

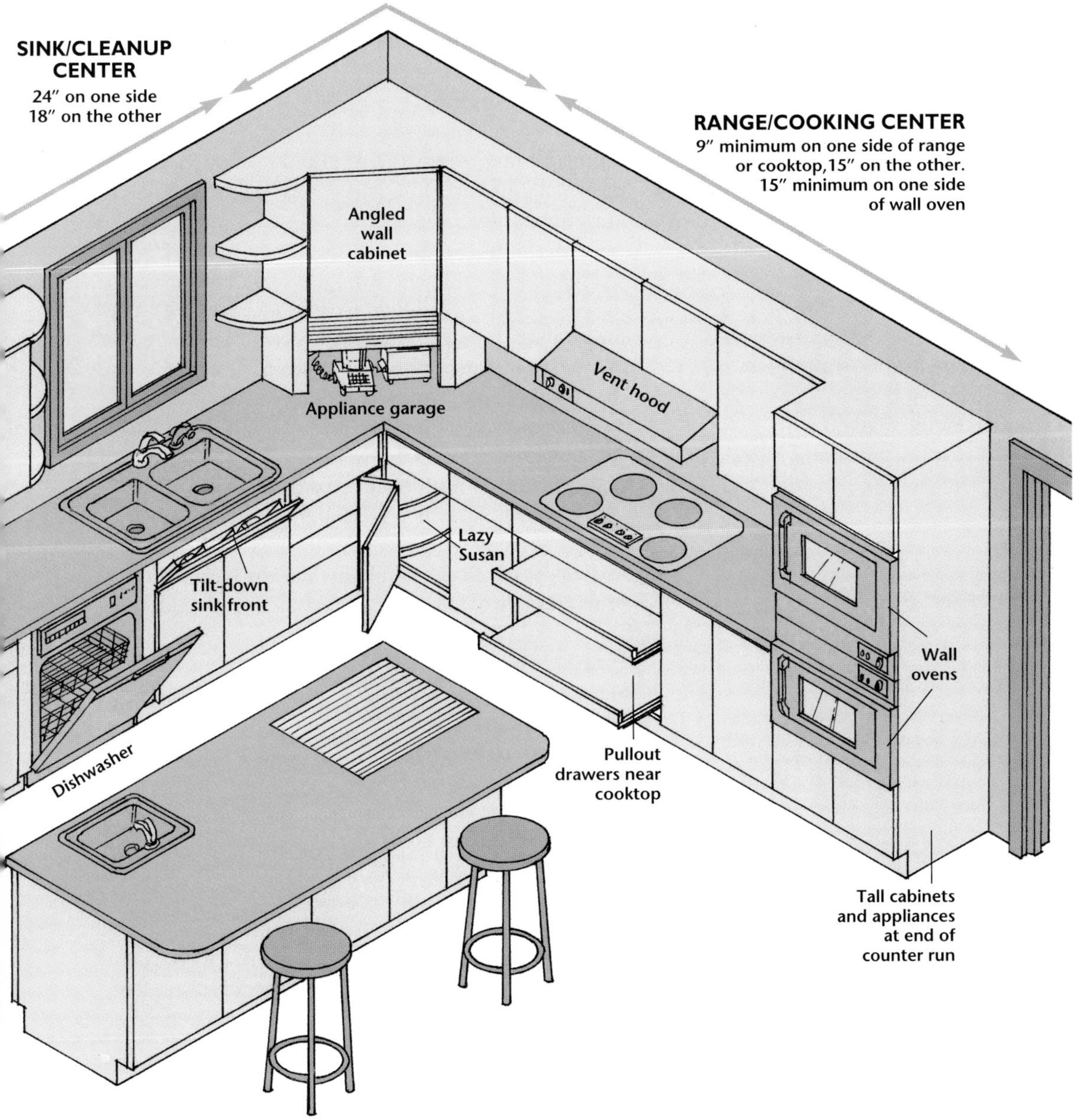

SINK/CLEANUP CENTER
24" on one side
18" on the other

RANGE/COOKING CENTER
9" minimum on one side of range
or cooktop,15" on the other.
15" minimum on one side
of wall oven

Angled wall cabinet

Appliance garage

Vent hood

Tilt-down sink front

Lazy Susan

Dishwasher

Pullout drawers near cooktop

Wall ovens

Tall cabinets and appliances at end of counter run

Though a microwave oven is thought of as part of the cooking center, many people prefer to situate it near the refrigerator/freezer or in the serving center. Depending on the model, microwave ovens can be mounted inside an oven cabinet, on the underside of a wall cabinet, or just below the countertop in a base cabinet run. The microwave can always sit on the counter if you have sufficient space.

Plan to store often used pots and pans in base cabinet pull-out drawers mounted on heavy-duty drawer guides.

FOOD PREPARATION/MIXING CENTER

This auxiliary center is ideally located between the refrigerator and sink; allow a minimum of 36 inches of continuous countertop at least 16 inches deep. If you plan to raise or lower countertop heights, the food preparation area is a good place to customize, as some tasks may require lower than standard-height countertops. A butcher-block insert for chopping is a great addition for all cooks, while a marble counter insert is a boon for the serious pastry chef.

Appliance garages with tambour or paneled doors neatly hide a collection of small appliances, such as a can opener, a coffee grinder, and a blender. Place the garage in a deep corner to provide maximum storage space. (If you place an electrical outlet in the recess, all you have to do is pull the appliance to the front of the garage and it's ready for use.) For immediate access to spices or staples, consider an open shelf or backsplash rack.

SERVING AREA (OPTIONAL)

If you have space, locate this optional work area between the range and sink. It can share space here with both the cleanup and cooking centers. You will need a minimum of 36 inches of countertop area. To determine the minimum counter space for two adjacent work centers, use the longer of the two required counter lengths and add 12 inches.

Everyday dishes, glassware, flatware, serving plates, and bowls, as well as napkins and placemats, belong in this area. The dishwasher should be nearby.

Once you've decided on a basic layout and blocked out the various work centers in your kitchen, it's time to fine-tune your floor plan. You'll need to mark all the details of the design you've worked out onto a scale drawing of your kitchen's perimeter.

It's also time to turn your attention to the walls. To do this, you may want to draw elevations of each wall, indicating the location and dimensions of all the elements in your kitchen.

If the layout of your kitchen is changing significantly, you may need to make adjustments in the room's heating, electrical, or plumbing systems, rerouting lines or adding new ones. Indicate on your plan where plumbing, gas, and electrical lines enter the room and how they'll reach the appliances.

Also, mark the tentative locations of electrical outlets, switches, and light fixtures (see pages 48–49 for more on lighting). Every countertop longer than 12 inches should have at least one two-plug outlet; most should have an outlet every 18 inches to four feet. In an area where you'll be storing and using small appliances, you may want to install a power strip with multiple outlets built in at equal distances.

If your first kitchen measurements were in feet and inches, you may now wish to convert them to inches—you'll find it simpler when working with professionals or shopping for cabinets and appliances.

HEIGHTS AND CLEARANCES

Standard minimum clearances have been established for kitchens to ensure enough space for both a busy cook and occasional foot traffic, enough door clearance for unhindered access to cabinets, dishwasher, and refrigerator, and traffic lanes wide enough for diners to comfortably enter and exit a breakfast nook.

Heights and clearances for a free-standing table and chairs, as well as an eating counter, are shown below. For a booth with seating on both sides, you will need a minimum width of 64 inches. Allow 15–18 inches of clearance between the edge of the table and the back of the bench, and 10–12 inches of clearance from the bench seat to the tabletop.

STANDARD CLEARANCES

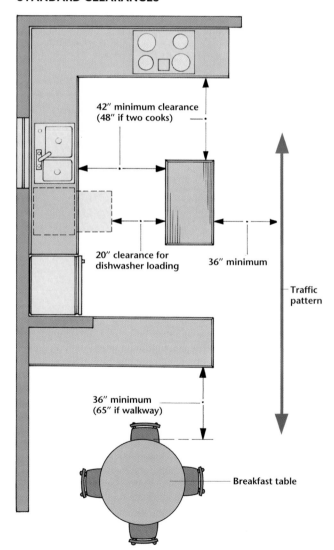

In a well-planned kitchen, standard minimum clearances (above) have been established to ensure enough space for a busy cook to work in and to entertain guests, for foot traffic through the kitchen, for doors and cabinets to open unhindered, and for diners to enter and sit down comfortably at the table.

STANDARD HEIGHTS

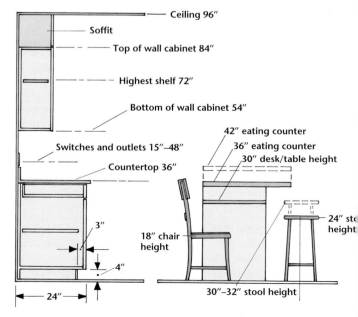

A KITCHEN ELEVATION

Elevation drawings are actually previews of the new arrangement of structural elements, appliances, and storage units. Because this preview is on paper, you can iron out the placement and proportions of various elements before you spend any money.

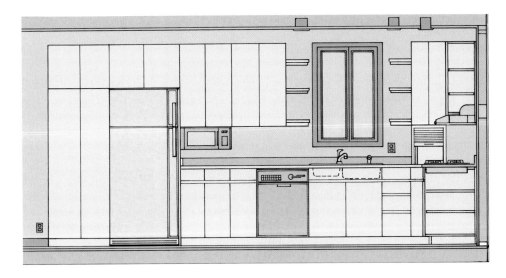

To visualize the new kitchen and spot possible problems, you can make cardboard cutouts to scale of both cabinets and appliances, use a design kit that comes with cutouts, or use kitchen design software to produce the layout and elevation on your computer. For planning purposes, allow a width of 36 inches for a refrigerator or a double-bowl sink, 24 inches for a dishwasher or a single-bowl sink, and 30 inches for a range or built-in cooktop. Place the cutouts on a tracing of your floor plan and check to see that your design meets the minimum clearances outlined in the drawing.

As you're working on your plan, think about the traffic pattern through the kitchen at different times of day and during parties. Trace the work triangle and door openings on a separate sheet of paper, indicating the traffic flow with arrows. To redirect traffic, try moving a door, angling a peninsula, or adding an island. Also check whether any appliance doors interfere with traffic. Now is the time to make the necessary changes on your plan.

CREATING ELEVATION DRAWINGS

To make elevation drawings, you'll need exact dimensions of all doors, windows, and appliances. It will also be necessary to work out storage details for each work center and decide on the heights of work surfaces, wall ovens, and hoods. For help, consult the drawing on the facing page, which gives standard heights and depths for base and wall cabinets and shelves, including heights for counters, stools, chairs, and desks and tables.

Work surfaces. The height of a work surface affects the height of the storage units that are above and below it. Depending on your height, a standard 36-inch-high counter may or may not be comfortable for you. If your elbow height (measuring from the floor) is less than the average 40 inches, you may want your countertops to be only 34 inches high; if your elbow height is more, consider making your counters higher. Though most appliances are manufactured to fit beneath or along a 36-inch-high counter, sinks and drop-in cooktops can be positioned at any height.

Even with standard cabinet heights, you may want to plan at least one lower or higher work surface. A pull-out board or an island that's at a different height from the rest of your counters would work, as would a butcher-block-top table on wheels.

Cabinetry. Most modular base and wall cabinets come in 3-inch increments (see pages 54–55 for detailed information on cabinetry). Exact measurements are essential, so it's a good idea to have your supplier check your final measurements on the site before you order your cabinets. If you run into a problem of fit, filler strips can be used between units or alongside a wall. You'll have to use filler strips in the corner if you choose cabinets without face frames. To keep costs down, you may want to buy a few wide cabinets rather than many narrow ones. Corners can pose a problem. Two cabinets that simply butt together waste valuable storage area. Some solutions include angled cabinets, blind cabinets, corner sinks, and lazy susans.

The soffit. You have choices for the soffit area, the space between a typical wall cabinet (84 inches at the top line) and the ceiling (96 inches or higher). You can simply leave the space open and use it to display china and collectibles, mounting them on the wall or protecting them behind a rail attached to the top of the cabinets. Or you can frame in the space with wallboard. Another choice is to build a box soffit over the wall cabinets for downlights, good for task lighting on countertops.

A range hood. Unless you're planning a downventing exhaust system, you need to install a hood over the cooktop or range. Local codes as well as manufacturers of hoods can give you the required hood width (based on the size of the cooktop) and height above the burners. (For information on your options, see page 60.) Check to see if the hood fits your cabinet run.

Designing your kitchen is a way of giving it personality and a way of expressing yourself. Your kitchen can be warm and homey, sleek and spare, or sophisticated and up-to-the-minute, whichever look best expresses your family's lifestyle. You can design a kitchen around a particular style or period such as Victorian or French country, taking clues from the other rooms in your house. You could create a theme based on a personal collection or a favorite motif, or let materials you like, such as stone, tile, or stainless steel, set the tone.

All the elements in your kitchen contribute to its design: the cabinets, the countertops, the walls and floor, the appliances, the ceiling and the lighting, the window treatments, the finishes, and all the details.

What makes a kitchen design successful? It is a kitchen that has visual impact, one that includes a creative mix of materials and, most of all, one that is efficient, easy to use, functional, and comfortable.

LINE, SHAPE, AND SCALE
Line, shape, and the proportion and arrangement of cabinets and appliances affect the visual space of a kitchen.

Line. Most kitchens incorporate many different types of lines but often one predominates in the design. Vertical lines give a sense of height, horizontal lines add width, diagonals suggest movement and give a sense of open space, and curved and angular lines impart a feeling of grace and dynamism.

Continuity of line gives a sense of unity to a design. Look at one of your elevation sketches. It's not necessary for everything to align perfectly, but making small changes in the width or height of a cabinet (without sacrificing storage) so it lines up with appliances or other cabinets can smooth out a design. At the same time, cabinets of different heights can break up a long horizontal line and add some energy.

Shape. Harmony of shapes is also important in achieving a unified design. Exact repetition can be monotonous, but a balanced arrangement of objects in the same shape, though of different sizes, creates a pleasing effect. Study the shapes created by doorways, windows, cabinets, and appliances. To create a sense of harmony you could repeat the arch over a cooking niche, for example, in a doorway or in the trim of an open shelf.

Scale. When the scale of the elements is proportionate to the overall scale of the room, the design appears harmonious. A small kitchen will seem even smaller with oversized appliances and closed cabinets. Open shelves and a simple design will visually enlarge such a room. Also, proportion affects adjacent elements. Small objects arranged in a group help balance a larger item, making it less obtrusive.

WORKING WITH COLOR
Color is an exciting, versatile, and easy-to-use design tool. The size of your kitchen, your personal preferences, and the mood you want to create all affect the selection of your color scheme. Here are some guidelines as you plan.

Warm and cool. A color's visual temperature can alter the sense of space in a room. Oranges, yellows, and other colors with a red tone impart a feeling of warmth, but they also contract space. Blues, greens, and other colors with a blue tone make an area seem cooler and larger. Light colors enlarge a space. Darker values absorb light and diminish a room or visually lower a ceiling.

Contrast. In a small kitchen, too much contrast has the same effect as a dark color—it reduces the sense of space. Contrasting colors work well for drawing attention to interesting structural elements. Accent colors used strategically can affect the sense of space. A bright color used sparingly on a backsplash or behind a shelf can give a feeling of depth. Using one color throughout an area helps to conceal a less than attractive feature.

A light, monochromatic color scheme (one that uses different shades of one color) is usually restful and serene. Contrasting colors, on the other hand, add vibrancy and excitement to a design but can be overpowering unless the tones of the colors are varied. It's a good idea to keep the appliances neutral and bring color into the room in other ways. If you like to change the decor of your rooms often,

About Style
Cabinets set the tone for a kitchen and can be designed to complement the style in the rest of your home. Some popular styles are listed below, but don't limit yourself to a convenient label, since most kitchens lend themselves to a combination of styles.

Traditional cabinets have the timeless look of Old World furniture, familiar and warm yet balanced, formal, and well-made, often of cherry, oak, or mahogany.

Contemporary is a sleek and smooth look characterized by clean lines and an absence of decoration. Materials used include laminates, glass, chrome, and some stone. The colors used are often pale.

High tech takes sleekness to an even greater extreme and is noted for its use of commercial building materials and industrial textures, including galvanized steel, concrete, and limestone.

Country cabinets evoke the warmth and casual feeling of an old farmhouse kitchen, using natural materials like plain wood in pine, oak, or maple.

In a windowless kitchen, charcoal gray cabinets and stainless steel appliances create a dramatic monochromatic look.

All white cabinets brighten a small space; a rolling worktable and whimsical wrought-iron chairs keep it uncluttered.

use bright colors as accents for furnishings and accessories that can be changed without too much trouble or cost.

Psychological effects. Colors often evoke a strong psychological response. White, gray, and tan are neutral colors that give a sense of serenity and simplicity. Pastel colors give a feeling of innocence, of being taken care of. Yellow is cheerful and is said to stimulate the appetite. Red is a hot color that entices people and is a great backdrop for food. Orange is full of life, combining yellow's cheerfulness with red's warmth. Blue signifies loyalty and contemplation, and creates a place of concentration. Purple is said, perhaps unjustly, to be a color that is difficult to work with and one that represses the appetite. Green brings nature indoors and is universally well liked. Black is sophisticated but suggests remoteness. Color is a powerful tool, so choose carefully.

ADDING TEXTURE AND PATTERN

Texture and pattern also define a room's space and style. The materials in a kitchen may include many different textures—from a shiny tiled backsplash to rough oak cabinets, from matte wallpaper to a glossy enameled sink, from coarse quarry tile flooring to smooth plastic laminate countertops. Using a variety of textures helps to avoid an austere look, but too much can be overwhelming. Let a strong feature or predominant pattern act as the focus of your design and choose other surfaces to complement it.

Rough textures absorb light, dull colors, and lend a feeling of informality. Smooth textures reflect light and can suggest elegance or modernity. Using similar textures helps unify a design and create a mood.

Pattern choices must also harmonize with the predominant style of the room. Though pattern is usually associated with wallpaper or some flooring, natural substances such as wood, brick, and stone also create patterns. Nevertheless, natural products generally work well with all textures and colors.

Fabrics used in window treatments, seat cushions, and area rugs provide another opportunity to add texture and pattern. They also absorb sound, important in a room with many hard surfaces.

CREATING A DESIGN BOARD

Before you commit to any design decisions, you will want to live with them. Create a design board, placing swatches of fabric, paint, tile, laminate color chips, and other samples on a piece of posterboard. Hang it in your kitchen and live with it for a while. Some paint companies now have paint chips that are at least 9 by 12 inches, or you can paint an entire piece of posterboard in the colors you contemplate using and live with them for a while.

Note also that the placement of light fixtures, and the kinds of bulbs used in them, will have an effect on the color in your kitchen. Make an effort to look at your design choices under the kind of light you have chosen. For details on lighting, see pages 48–49.

A room comes alive with light. And proper kitchen lighting, working in tandem with a good layout and modern fixtures, creates a safe and pleasant place to work. A good lighting plan provides shadowless, glarefree illumination for the entire room as well as bright, uniform light for specific tasks. If you plan to dine and entertain in the kitchen, you'll also want to be able to vary the levels of lighting for a softer, more dramatic mood.

The best kitchen lighting is not only highly functional but also adds visual interest. The key to successful kitchen lighting is using the right kinds of light in the right combination. Because electrical fittings have to be installed before the cabinets and appliances, you have to decide at an early stage of the kitchen design where in the room you will want fixtures.

THE COLOR OF LIGHT

When deciding what kinds of fixtures to install in your kitchen, consider the color light that the different bulbs emit.

Incandescent bulbs have the warmest light—a pleasant reddish-yellow that makes skin tones look good, makes the colors of food look inviting, and is comfortable to work under.

Fluorescent tubes emit a cooler blue or blue-white light. Formerly, fluorescent bulbs were criticized for their poor color rendition, giving off a somewhat greenish-blue light. Now the tubes are available in a variety of colors usually described as warm white, soft white, and daylight. However, the light is still cooler than that of incandescents.

Halogen bulbs emit the whitest light, closest to natural sunlight.

THREE KINDS OF LIGHTING

Today's designers describe three specific kinds of lighting: ambient, task, and accent.

Ambient or general lighting fills a room with a soft level of light; it's usually the light you turn on when you walk into the room. How much light you need depends on the color as well as the size of the room. Dark colors absorb light; light colors reflect it.

Task lighting illuminates a particular area where you need to perform a task, making the work easier and safer. Task lighting is directed at individual work areas and prevents shadows. It can be installed above the sink, over the stove (some range hoods come with lights), under the upper cabinets, above an island, or over an eating area.

Accent lighting, primarily decorative, is used to highlight an architectural feature, set a mood, or provide drama. Accent lights can be placed on top of upper cabinets directed at the ceiling, in the toe-kick space of lower cabinets for a whimsical touch, or on the inside edge of cabinets with glass doors to highlight the contents.

LIGHT FIXTURES

There are a variety of choices in light fixtures specifically designed to enhance your various activities in the kitchen.

Recessed downlights, or cans, are popular and unobtrusive for general lighting. Available as small as 4 inches wide, they look like small circles in the ceiling. For best illumination, place the lights close enough together so their light patterns overlap, and at least two feet (counter depth) away from a wall.

Surface-mounted lights, once the only kitchen lights, still work well, especially in kitchens that cannot accommodate recessed fixtures. Available in many styles and sizes, there are fixtures for either incandescent or fluorescent bulbs.

Pendant lights or hanging lights can be placed above a counter, an island, or a dining table. A pendant that can be raised or lowered is very adaptable. A chandelier, a multiple-arm pendant light, works well over a table, creating lighting for dining. Position a pendant 30 to 36 inches above a counter and at a comfortable height above the head.

Undercabinet lighting is mounted under upper cabinets behind cabinet trim. Usually a narrow fluorescent strip, undercabinet lighting can also be small incandescent bulbs or the newer strips of small round halogen lights called puck lights.

Track lighting has become slimmer and sleeker and more adaptable. Place the lamps close together to form general lighting or aim them at specific areas for spotlighting. Open tracks are more flexible, allowing lights to be moved anywhere along the channel. Closed channels are easier to clean, but once fixtures are placed they cannot be moved. Cable lighting, track lighting that's narrowed down to two thin parallel cords, can be fitted with many different contemporary fixtures.

DIMMERS

Dimmers, also called rheostats, enable you to set a fixture at any level of light from a soft glow to a radiant brightness, thus allowing for a variety of moods in the kitchen. Dimmers are also energy savers. It's easy and inexpensive to install a dimmer for incandescent bulbs. The initial cost of dimmers for fluorescents is higher, and the variety of fixtures is limited. Dimmers can be round knobs that rotate or a toggle switch or a slide bar that moves up and down.

PLACING FIXTURES ON YOUR FLOOR PLAN

When you have decided where and how many light fixtures you want, draw them on your floor plan, showing which switch operates which light source and indicate whether it is single, a multiple, or a dimmer. Plan to add a three- or four-way switch if your kitchen has more than one entrance. Place switches 44 inches above the floor on the handle side of doorways.

Lightbulbs and tubes

INCANDESCENT

Incandescent light, the kind used most often in our homes, is produced by a tungsten thread that burns slowly inside a glass bulb. A-bulbs are traditional, R and PAR produce a more controlled beam, and silvered bulbs diffuse light.

Low-voltage incandescent fixtures make good accent lighting. Operating on 12 or 24 volts, these lights require transformers, which are sometimes built into the fixtures, to step down the voltage from standard 120-volt household circuits. Low-voltage fixtures are relatively expensive to buy but are energy- and cost-efficient in the long run.

FLUORESCENT

Fluorescent tubes, unrivaled for energy efficiency and lasting far longer than incandescent bulbs, are sometimes required by building codes for new kitchens. Older fluorescent tubes were slow to start, noisy, flickered, and had poor color rendition. Newer tubes, with rapid-start features, electronic ballasts, and better fixture shielding for noise and flicker, come in a wide spectrum of colors. New subcompact tubes can be used in fixtures that usually require incandescent bulbs.

HALOGEN

Quartz halogen lights are bright white light good for task and accent lighting. Halogen is usually low voltage but may use standard line current. The popular MR-16 bulb creates the tightest beam while the PAR-36 bulb has a longer reach and wider coverage.

Halogen has two disadvantages: its initial high cost and its very high heat. Be sure to choose a fixture specifically designed for halogen bulbs.

COMPARING LIGHTBULBS AND TUBES

A-Bulb
Description. Familiar pear shape; frosted or clear.
Uses. Everyday household use.

T-Tubular
Description. Tube-shaped, from 5" long. Frosted or clear.
Uses. Cabinets, decorative fixtures.

R-Reflector
Description. White or silvered coating directs light out end of funnel-shaped bulb.
Uses. Directional fixtures; focuses light where needed.

PAR-Parabolic aluminized reflector
Description. Similar to auto headlamps; special shape and coating project light and control beam.
Uses. Recessed downlights and track fixtures.

Silvered bowl
Description. A-bulb, with silvered cap to cut glare and produce indirect light.
Uses. Track fixtures and pendants.

Low-voltage strip
Description. Like Christmas tree lights; in strips or tracks, or encased in flexible, waterproof plastic.
Uses. Task lighting and decoration.

Tube
Description. Tube-shaped, 5" to 96" long. Needs special fixture and ballast.
Uses. Shadowless work light; also indirect lighting.

PL-Compact tube
Description. U-shaped with base; 5¼" to 7½" long.
Uses. In recessed downlights; some PL tubes include ballasts to replace A-bulbs.

Subcompact
Description. Twister, bullet, or bulb shaped with the same screw-type base as an incandescent bulb.
Uses. In lamps and fixtures that usually take an incandescent bulb.

High intensity
Description. Small, clear bulb with consistently high light output; used in halogen fixtures only.
Uses. Specialized task lamps, torchères, and pendants.

Low-voltage MR-16— (mini-reflector)

Description. Tiny (2"-diameter) project bulb; gives small circle of light from a distance.
Uses. Low-voltage track fixtures, mono-spots, and recessed downlights.

Low-voltage PAR

Description. Similar to auto headlight; tiny filament, shape, and coating give precise direction.
Uses. To project a small spot of light a long distance.

Universal design

All of us are young once, most of us become old, and any of us can become disabled at any time. And as we age, our capabilities change. A kitchen design that considers the needs of all people who will use it—children, the elderly, and handicapped people—is called a universal design.

Universal design accommodates a wide range of individual preferences and abilities, and is most successful when it can be used efficiently and comfortably without great effort, when it minimizes hazards, and incorporates user-friendly materials.

This universally designed kitchen has knee space under the sink, a raised dishwasher, and counters of varying heights.

For More Information
For more information about universal design, you can contact the following organizations.

Adaptive Environments Center, Inc.
374 Congress St., Suite 301, Boston, MA 02210
(617) 695-1225
www.adaptenv.org

The Center for Universal Design
School of Design
North Carolina State University
Box 8613, Raleigh, NC 27695-8613
(800) 647-6777
www.ncsu.edu/ncsu/design/cud

GUIDELINES
Many of the general recommendations for kitchen heights and clearances (see pages 44–45) now reflect universal guidelines, but there are some things to consider. Some of the following accommodations for a universal kitchen have to do with the placement of the kitchen elements, others with their design.

- Doorways at least 32 inches wide
- Aisles at least 42 inches wide for one cook, 48 inches wide for two cooks
- A center space of 5 by 5 feet for a turnaround
- Countertops 29 to 32 inches high and 27 to 30 inches deep so a chair or wheelchair can fit underneath
- Countertops with a matte finish to reduce glare
- Rounded corners on any open counters
- A wall oven at a comfortable height rather than a range
- A cooking surface with control knobs at the front or side
- A landing space at least 15 inches wide next to the cooking surface and one next to or directly across from a microwave or oven
- A ventilation system with a fan rated at a minimum of 150 CFM (see page 60)
- A dishwasher raised 18 to 30 inches off the floor to minimize bending and for easier access
- A side-by-side refrigerator with pull-out shelves for easy access to both refrigerator and freezer
- Faucets with paddle-style handles and an antiscald device
- Wall cabinets with shallow shelves placed no higher than 15 inches above the countertop
- Open shelving
- Frequently used items stored 15 to 48 inches off the floor (or approximately knee to shoulder height)
- Door handles, faucet handles, and cabinet hardware replaced with levers and pulls that can be operated with one hand
- Slip-resistant flooring
- Light switches, electrical outlets, and thermostats no higher than 40 to 42 inches off the floor
- Light switches that slide up and down

SAFETY
A universal kitchen is also one that is safe to work in. Your kitchen should have ground-fault circuit interrupters (GFCI) for all electrical receptacles (see page 81), a fire extinguisher in a visible location, and smoke alarms installed nearby.

Once you have worked out an efficient layout, planned your storage requirements, and decided on color and lighting schemes, you will make your final decisions regarding new appliances, cabinets and countertops, and flooring (for help, see pages 54–63).

Then you will want to decide on the finishing touches of the design, draw a new floor plan, order materials, set up a schedule for the work, review your insurance policies, and find out about building codes and permits before you begin the work.

FINISHING TOUCHES

The finishing touches make the difference in any room and deserve careful attention. This is the time to choose all the hardware for the cabinets—doorknobs, drawer pulls, and hinges—as well as decide on moldings, curtains, and blinds. All these details help pull the design together and make the statement more personal.

DRAWING A NEW FLOOR PLAN

Draw your new floor plan, or working drawing, the same way you did the existing plan, with paper and a ruler or using kitchen design software for your computer (see pages 38–39). On the new plan, include existing features you want to preserve and all the changes you're planning to make. If you prefer, you can hire a designer, drafter, or contractor to draw the final plan for you.

For more complicated projects, the building department may require additional or more detailed drawings showing structural, plumbing, and wiring changes. You may also need to show areas adjacent to the kitchen so building officials can determine how the project will affect the rest of your house. Elevation sketches are not required, but they'll prove helpful in planning the work.

The vibrant red of the range is repeated in an accent line of small square tiles above the counter, as well as in the light fixtures, and the owner's choice of pots and pans.

The family pet was not forgotten in this kitchen remodel. A cozy spot was incorporated into the granite-topped island.

ORDERING MATERIALS

If you do the ordering of materials for your remodeling project, you'll need to compile a detailed master list. Not only will this launch your work, but it will also help you keep track of purchases and deliveries. For each item, specify the following information: name and model or serial number, manufacturer, source of material, date of order, expected delivery date, color, size or dimensions, quantity, price (including tax and delivery charge), and a second choice just in case one is needed.

Ordering materials will also help you set up a schedule for the project. This is also a good time to review your insurance policies to see what aspects of the job are covered, check that you are within your budget, and decide where you will set up temporary quarters for eating and cooking.

OBTAINING BUILDING PERMITS

To discover which building codes may affect your remodeling project and whether a building permit is required, check with your city or county building department.

You may need to apply for one or more permits: structural, plumbing, mechanical heating or cooling, reroofing, or electrical. More complicated projects sometimes require that the design and the working drawings be executed by an architect, designer, or state-licensed contractor.

For your permit you'll be charged either a flat fee or a percentage of the estimated cost of materials and labor. You may also have to pay a fee to have someone check the plans.

If you're acting as your own contractor, it's your responsibility to ask the building department to inspect the work as it progresses. Failure to obtain a permit or an inspection may result in your having to dismantle completed work.

Working with professionals

Major kitchen remodeling projects are not easy work, so you will want to evaluate your do-it-yourself skills. If you know how to draw plans but dislike physical labor, you'll need someone to perform the actual construction. If you're able to wield a saw and hammer but can't draw, you can hire a professional to prepare working drawings. Or you can let professionals handle all the tasks, from drawing plans through applying the finishing touches.

Hiring the right professional for the job need not be daunting. No matter whom you consult, be as precise as possible about what you want. Collect photographs from magazines, brochures, and advertisements. Describe exactly what materials you want to use. Provide a preliminary plan and some idea of your budget. Write down any questions you have as you think of them. The more information you can supply, the better job a professional will be able to do for you.

A kitchen remodel is more than just a construction project; it's a personal project, a reflection of your home and an expression of your family's identity. In choosing a professional, look not only for someone who is technically and artistically skilled but also for someone with whom you and your family feel comfortable.

ARCHITECT OR DESIGNER?

Either an architect or a designer can draw plans acceptable to building department officials; each can send out bids, help you select a contractor, and supervise the contractor's performance to ensure that your plans and time schedule are being followed. Some architects and designers even double as their own contractors.

Most states do not require designers to be licensed, as architects must be; designers may charge less for their labor. Architects can do stress calculations, if these are needed; designers need state-licensed engineers to design the structure and sign the working drawings.

Kitchen designers are specially trained and know about the latest building materials and techniques. An interior designer specializes in decorating and furnishing of rooms and can be hired for the finishing touches. They both can offer fresh, innovative ideas and advice. Through their contacts you have access to materials not available at the retail level.

Architects and designers may or may not charge for time spent in an exploratory interview. For plans, you'll probably be charged on an hourly basis. If an architect or designer selects the contractor and keeps an eye on

An enlarged pass-through over the sink allows light from the enclosed porch windows to flood the kitchen. The opening's wood frame has a verdigris finish that complements the gray and beige granite countertops and the charming green light fixtures.

construction, plan to pay either an hourly rate or a percentage of the cost of materials and labor—15 to 25 percent is typical. Descriptions of the services and amount of the charges should be stated in advance in writing to prevent later expensive misunderstandings.

CHOOSING A CONTRACTOR

Contractors do more than construction. Often, they can draw plans acceptable to building department officials and can obtain building permits. A contractor's experience and technical know-how may end up saving you money.

To find a contractor, ask architects, designers, and friends for recommendations. Compare bids from at least three state-licensed contractors, giving each one either an exact description and sketches of the desired remodeling, or plans and specifications prepared by an architect or designer. Include a detailed account of who will be responsible for what work.

Don't make your decision on price alone; reliability, quality of work, and on-time performance are also important. Ask the contractors for the names and phone numbers of their clients. Call several and ask them about the contractor's performance and then inspect the work, both a finished project and one in progress, if possible. Check bank and credit references to determine the contractor's financial responsibility. Make sure the contractor has insurance. Don't hire someone who rushes to talk about payment before any work is done, is hesitant to give references, or is late. The relationship of contractor and client is crucial to a successful project. Both must understand the other's needs, be open to communication, and, most of all, trust each other. Good rapport is important to the success of any job.

Though some contractors may want a fee based on a percentage of the cost of materials and labor, it's usually wiser to insist on a fixed-price bid. This protects you against both a rise in the cost of materials (assuming that the contractor does the buying) and the chance that the work will take more time, adding to your labor costs. Many states limit the amount of "good faith" money that contractors can require before work begins. Don't underestimate the time it will take to do the work.

HIRING SUBCONTRACTORS

When you act as your own general contractor and put various parts of your project out to bid with subcontractors, you must use the same care you'd exercise in hiring a general contractor.

You'll need to check references, financial resources, and insurance coverage of a number of subcontractors. Once you've received bids and chosen your sub-contractors, work out a detailed contract for each specific job and carefully supervise all the work.

Who's Who

Many of the professionals involved with home remodeling belong to organizations that certify that they are licensed in their field. These organizations can answer questions and provide information to the homeowner.

AIA—The American Institute of Architects

This is the national professional organization
for licensed (by the state) architects.
1735 New York Ave.
Washington, DC 20006
(202) 626-7300
www.aiaonline.com

AIBD—American Institute of Building Design

Award is Professional Building Designer (PBD).
991 Post Rd. East
Westport, CT 06880
(800) 366-2423 or (203) 227-3640
www.aibd.org

ASID—The American Society of Interior Designers

Membership is based on education, experience, and testing by the National Council for Interior Design Qualifications.
608 Massachusetts Ave. NE
Washington, DC 20002
(202) 546-3480
www.asid.org

NAHB—National Association of Home Builders

Certifies educational and managerial standards.
Award is Certified Graduate Remodeler (CGR).
1201 15th St. NW
Washington, DC 20005
(800) 368-5242, ext. 216, or (202) 822-0216
www.nahb.com

NARI—National Association of the Remodeling Industry

Award is Certified Remodeler (CR).
4900 Seminary Rd., Suite 320
Alexandria, VA 22311
(703) 575-1100
www.nari.org

NKBA—National Kitchen & Bath Association

Qualified professionals are Certified Kitchen Designers (CKD).
687 Willow Grove St.
Hackettstown, NJ 07840
(800) 367-6522 or (908) 852-0033
www.nkba.com

Cabinets

Cabinets help determine a kitchen's personality and in a new kitchen represent the biggest part of the overall cost. You want to choose carefully. If your cabinets are in good condition, you may want to consider refacing them as a less expensive way to achieve a completely new look (see page 92).

The wide range of available styles and sizes allows you great freedom to create your choice of decor. Careful attention to construction and materials should be your first consideration. Check on such details as an interior finish that is easy to clean, doweled joints (not glued or pinned), corner supports, drawer guides, shelving options, self-closing hinges, catches, and comfortable pulls. Make sure laminates and edge banding are thick enough not to peel at the corners and edges.

You can buy ready-to-assemble kits, stock, custom, or modular cabinets. Ready-to-assemble kits (RTA) come with all the parts and hardware and cost the least because you assemble them yourself using a screwdriver or wrench. They offer the fewest design choices. Mass-produced, standard-sized stock units are typically the least expensive option for ready-made cabinets and can

be an excellent choice if you clearly understand your needs. Custom shops can match old cabinets, build to odd configurations, and accommodate details that aren't handled by stock cabinets, although this is generally a more expensive approach. A new hybrid, the custom modular cabinet, is manufactured but offers greater design flexibility than stock. Not surprisingly, modular cabinets cost more, too; you place an order and wait.

CABINET CONSTRUCTION

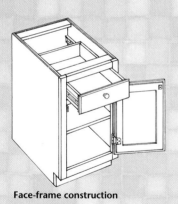

Face-frame construction

The durability of a cabinet depends on the type and thickness of the materials used and the quality of construction. The two basic cabinet construction styles are **face frame** and **frameless**. Traditional American cabinets mask the raw front edges of each box with a 1- by 2-inch face frame. On European, or frameless, cabinets, a simple narrow trim strip covers raw edges; doors and drawers usually fit to within ¼ inch of each other, revealing a thin sliver of the trim. Door hinges are invisible. Most are built with columns of holes drilled every 32 millimeters on the inside frame so interchangeable components fit together, making frameless cabinets very versatile.

Frameless cabinets allow for better access and increased storage space.

Cabinet door style, along with the choice of material and finish, determine the cabinet's look as well as the cost. One way to break up a long line of cabinets is to mix and match the doors, adding an area of glass doors or doors with decorative inserts of beadboard or punched tin. Or add areas of open shelving, plate racks, or wine racks. Also staggering the heights of the cabinets can add visual interest. To create a built-in look, you can add panels that match the cabinets to appliances and attach molding to cabinets, available from most larger manufacturers.

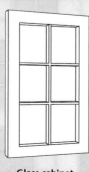

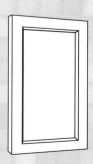

Frameless construction

Raised cabinet door   **Glass cabinet door**   **Beaded cabinet door**   **Recessed cabinet door**

Sink base

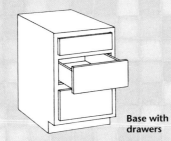

Base with drawers

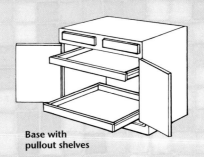

Base with pullout shelves

BASE CABINETS

Base cabinets do double duty, combining storage space with a working surface. Some base cabinets have one drawer over one or a pair of doors; others have multiple drawers and no doors. Sink units have a false drawer front at the top or a tilt-out panel for sponges and scouring pads.

Standard dimensions are 24 inches deep by 34½ inches high; the addition of a countertop raises them to 36 inches. In width, base cabinets range from 9 to 60 inches, increasing in increments of 3 inches from 9 to 36 inches and in increments of 6 inches after that.

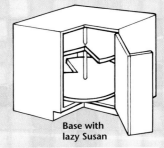

Base with lazy Susan

WALL CABINETS

Usually mounted on walls, these cabinets can also be hung from the ceiling for peninsula and island installation. Wall cabinets come in singles, doubles, and various specialty configurations. Typically 12 or 15 inches deep, cabinets can vary in width from 9 to 60 inches. The most frequently used heights are 15, 18, and 30 inches, but units range from 12 to 36 inches high or more. The shorter cabinets are typically mounted above refrigerators, ranges, or sinks.

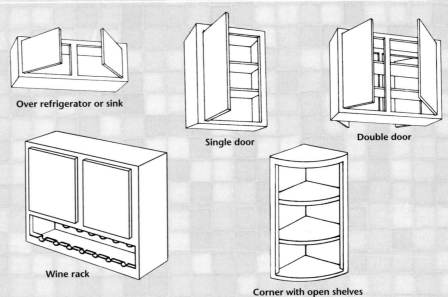

Over refrigerator or sink

Single door

Double door

Wine rack

Corner with open shelves

SPECIAL USE CABINETS

Manufacturers produce a variety of special-purpose cabinets. You can buy cabinets for built-in ranges, and microwave or slide-in ovens. Island and pantry units also fall into this category. Before purchasing expensive custom cabinets, look into stock cabinets that can be modified with pull-out boards, turn-around or slide-out shelves, and storage for small appliances.

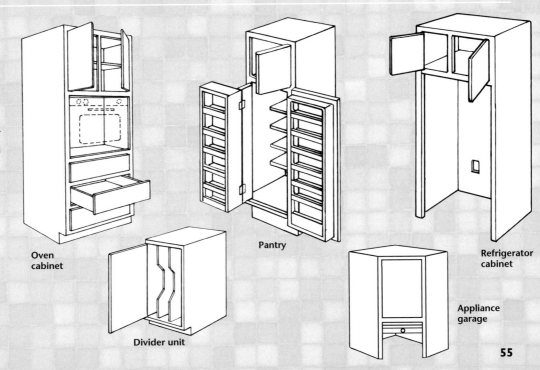

Oven cabinet

Pantry

Refrigerator cabinet

Divider unit

Appliance garage

Sinks and faucets

Your choice of sink will depend on the amount of counter space you have, how many people will be using it, and the look you like. Most commercially available sinks come with holes drilled for faucets, sprayers, or hot water dispensers.

Sinks can be mounted in several ways. A self-rimmed sink has a molded overlap and rests on the edge of the countertop cutout. A rimmed sink has a flat rim with surrounding metal strips to hold the basin to the countertop. A flush mount is used to attach a sink with squared-off corners even with the countertop, usually a tile surface. An undermounted sink, unrimmed and with metal clips to hold it in place, is installed below a countertop made of solid surfacing or stone.

Common sink materials include stainless steel, enameled cast iron or steel, solid surfacing, and composites. With stainless steel, look for a matte finish 18-gauge chromium/nickel blend with an undercoating for durability, easy upkeep, and less noise. Enameled cast-iron sinks have a heavier layer of baked-on enamel than enameled steel, making them quieter and less likely to chip. Solid-surfacing sinks can be purchased as a sink alone or as an integral sink with a countertop. Composites, made of chipped quartz or granite embedded in resin, are expensive and look similar to enamel but are more durable and easier to clean. Porcelain is emerging as an elegant but costly choice.

Single. A single sink is usually 22 by 25 inches and can range in depth from a typical 7 or 8 inches up to 9 or 10 inches. When buying a single sink, look for one that is the largest your countertop allows.

Self-rimmed

Flush mount

Self-rimmed with disposer

Apron. This modern adaptation of a farmhouse sink is large and rectangular and finished on all sides. It rests on a cabinet with its front exposed.

Double. A double sink typically measures 22 by 33 inches overall and can have two sinks of equal or unequal size as well as an integrated drainboard. A double sink is the most popular model.

Double sink with steel deck

Apron sink

Triple. Triple models usually have a small center compartment that may house a garbage disposal. Accessories include a custom-made colander, cutting board, or dish drainer.

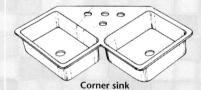
Triple sink with cutting board

Corner. Specially made to fit into a corner, this sink has two bowls at a 90-degree angle with the holes for faucet and handles in the space between them.

Corner sink

Integral. A sink and countertop all in one, made of stainless steel, solid-surface material, granite, or a composite concrete, is sleek looking and easy to clean because there are no seams or edges.

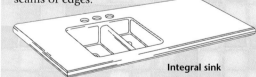
Integral sink

FAUCETS

Faucets can be center set, with hot and cold valves and spout connected in one unit; set widespread, with all three fixtures separate; or set as a single lever, with faucet and valves in one piece. Finishes include polished chrome, brushed chrome, nickel, polished or antiqued brass, pewter, gold, and enameled epoxy. For durability and low maintenance, solid-brass construction with a polished chrome surface having high nickel content is best.

Single-lever

Gooseneck with individual handles

Single-lever with pull-out sprayer

Dishwashers

In 1994 the U.S. Department of Energy revised the standards for dishwashers, reducing the amount of energy they could use. Manufacturers responded by designing models that use less water (since close to 80 percent of the energy used is to heat the water), have better filters, more insulation, and quieter pumps and motors. Some models have no center water tower, leaving more space for dishes. Features include booster heaters to heat the water above the temperature that comes from the hot water faucet, delayed start and pause buttons, and electronic touchpad control panels. The newest models have sensors to determine how dirty the dishes are, eliminating the need for different wash cycles. Available styles now include dishwasher drawers with separate washing mechanisms in each.

Both built-in and portable models are 24 inches wide, 24 inches deep, and 34 inches high. Interiors are either stainless steel, plastic-coated steel, or porcelain. Stainless steel interiors are reliable, don't chip or rust, and retain heat best. Interior racks should be sturdy and well balanced. Newer ones are made of a tough nylon. Look for a rack configuration that gives you the largest interior space for your dishes.

Built-in dishwashers fit under the countertop between two base cabinets. Finished on the front only, they are loaded from the front. When installed at the end of a cabinet run, side panels can be added. Front panels can be added to many models to coordinate with kitchen cabinets. For ease of use and to lessen back strain, dishwashers can be raised up. The National Kitchen and Bath Association (NKBA) recommends installing a dishwasher 9 to 12 inches off the floor.

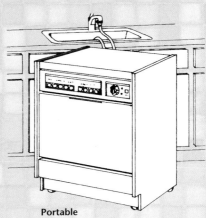

Portable units come with casters and hoses for attaching to sinks. Some have a hookup system that allows use of the faucet while the dishwasher is in operation. Newer models designed for later conversion to built-in are front loading.

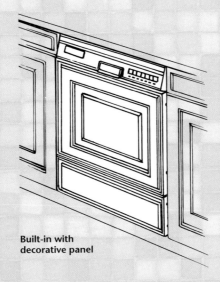

Built-in with decorative panel

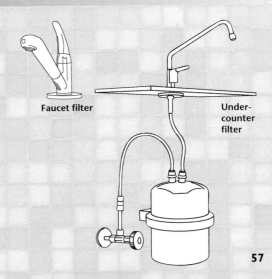

Portable

Water filters

Many water problems are nuisances rather than health hazards. But if you suspect a problem, have your water tested, then choose the right system for you. Any filter you buy should state that it is NSF (National Sanitation Foundation) certified.

An oxidizing filter helps remove iron. An activated-carbon filter removes the taste of heavily chlorinated water and clears the water of particles. The carbon or charcoal filters need to be replaced regularly. A sediment filter is a fine screen that traps particles and is usually used with an activated-carbon filter. A carbon filter can be mounted on the faucet, placed on the countertop next to the faucet, or installed on the pipe under the sink with a spigot at the sink.

A reverse-osmosis filter removes the same elements as a charcoal filter plus harmful chemicals. It is large and is installed under the sink by a professional.

Faucet filter

Under-counter filter

Cooktops

A cooktop, gas or electric, is built into a counter like a sink, with connections underneath. Cooktops are usually 30 or 36 inches wide, less than 3 inches deep, and 2 or 3 inches shorter than the standard 24-inch cabinet depth. Downventing models are about 16 inches deep. A standard cooktop has four burners, but five, six, or eight are available, as are pairs of burners that can be installed separately.

GAS

Gas is fast and efficient; it heats up quickly, is easy to control, and is inexpensive to use. Gas heat is measured in BTUs. The greater the range of BTUs in the burners, the more flexibility in cooking. Look for a cooktop with one or more heavy-duty burners. All new gas units have pilotless ignition, and some have automatic reignition. Sealed burners are more efficient and easier to clean.

Downventing gas

ELECTRIC

Traditional electric cooktops have four exposed coil burners in two different sizes. Electric burners heat and cool slowly, and retain their heat after being turned off. Solid-element units have sealed cast-iron plates over the coils. Electric heat is measured in watts.

Smoothtops. Electric cooktops with ceramic glass over the coils are sleek looking, easy to clean (although they may require a special cleaner), and require flat-bottomed pans for cooking. The heating elements may be radiant, coiled wires, or ribbons that glow red when heated; halogen, which uses a halogen bulb for heating; or magnetic induction, which heats a pan (a magnetic metal such as iron or steel, not aluminum) using an electromagnetic field.

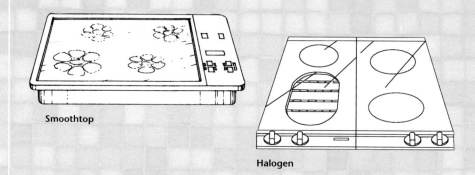

Smoothtop

Halogen

Commercial.
Commercial. Made of heavy-duty cast iron or fabricated metal, commercial gas units are available with as few as one or as many as eight burners and often come with hot plates or griddles. Commercial models are usually 6 to 7 inches high with short legs for installing on a base of tile or brick or other noncombustible material.

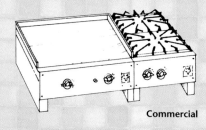

Commercial

MODULAR

Interchangeable plug-in modules allow for custom cooktops. A standard gas or electric burner can be removed and replaced with a grill, a griddle, a wok, or other specialty items. Mix-and-match modules go a step further: they can be grouped together with connecting hardware or embedded in the countertop separately. Typical modules are 12 inches wide.

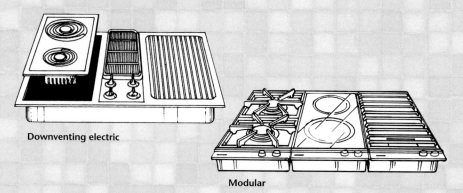

Downventing electric

Modular

Wall ovens

Built-in ovens combine with cooktops for a complete cooking package that allows you to choose which features you want most. As with ranges, you have the choice of traditional radiant, convection, or microwave. Double ovens, installed above one another or placed side by side, often combine a traditional radiant-heat oven with a microwave or a convection oven. An oven with a dark interior hides dirt and radiates more heat than one with light walls. Your oven can be one you clean yourself; one that provides continuous-cleaning, a slow process in which the oven cleans whenever it is turned on, (with results that may never look clean); or self-cleaning (pyrolitic), with a separate high-heat cleaning cycle during which the oven is locked and cannot be used for cooking.

RADIANT

Traditional radiant-heat ovens, also called thermal ovens, have gas or electric heat radiated from the bottom and/or top of the oven cavity. Available as single or double units, the most common widths are 24, 27, and 30 inches. More important though are the dimensions of the interior cavity. Measure to be sure there is room for things like cookie sheets or a Thanksgiving turkey, and opt for the largest interior cavity.

Oven options include digital timing devices, rotisseries, attached meat probes, and built-in warming shelves.

30" single with window

Single with window and rotisserie

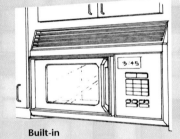

Built-in

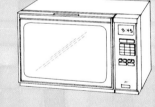

Countertop

MICROWAVE

In a microwave, foods cook quickly with high-frequency microwaves, but they don't brown. Some models offer a separate browning element; other built-in units combine microwave with radiant or convection cooking. Sizes range from subcompacts (.5 cubic foot) to full size (1 cubic foot or larger). Most useful are full-sized models with a minimum of 800 to 1,000 watts. Units can be placed on a counter, built into cabinetry, or purchased as part of a double wall oven or double-oven range.

Some microwaves, specially designed to be installed above a range (underneath wall cabinets), incorporate a vent and cooking lights; these are wider (30 inches) and shallower (13 to 17 inches deep). Some cooks feel these units are potentially hazardous when the burners below are in use.

Special features include touch controls, a memory bank, programmable cooking, timers, a temperature probe, rotisserie, and electronic sensors.

CONVECTION

Both gas and electric convection ovens use a fan to circulate hot air around the oven cavity. More energy-efficient than radiant-heat ovens, they can cut cooking time by 30 percent and use reduced temperatures. However, individual recipes have to be experimented with to determine the correct time and temperature. So-called "true convection" models have heating elements and fans placed outside the oven cavity to provide even results.

Convection ovens are great for roasting and baking (they first caught on in commercial bakeries) but are less effective for foods cooked in deep or covered dishes like cakes, stews, and casseroles. Some cooks feel that convection heat dries out certain foods, although in most models if convection heat is not needed, the fan can be turned off.

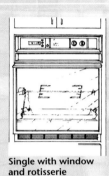

Convection with meat probe

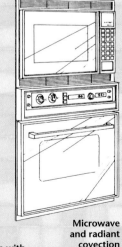

Microwave and radiant covection

Ranges and hoods

A range, or what many call a stove, is a combination of an oven and a cooktop and is available in a wide range of styles. Additional features include a broiler, drawer, and a backsplash. Three types of ranges include freestanding, slide-in (freestanding without side panels to fit between cabinets), and built-in (which sits on a base). To simplify cleaning of the cooktop, look for models with a minimum of seams.

Unless your range is downventing, you will need a hood over the cooktop. Ducted hoods channel odors, smoke, heat, and moisture from the kitchen to the outside; ductless hoods draw out some smoke and grease through a charcoal filter. The effectiveness of ventilation depends on the hood's capacity, the power of the fan or blower (blowers are quieter and more efficient), and the ductwork routing.

A freestanding range, with burners above the oven, rests on the floor; some slide in between cabinets. A few units offer a microwave oven above, with a built-in ventilator or downventing cooktop. Electric ranges may have coil or smooth cooktops and radiant or convection/radiant ovens. Gas ranges have either radiant or convection ovens.

Standard width is 30 inches; a 36-inch-wide (gas) or 40-inch-wide (electric) model offers greater flexibility. New features include reigniting gas burners, burner options such as a griddle or a bridge burner that lets two burners function as one, digital oven temperature displays, and delayed-time cooking.

Electric single oven

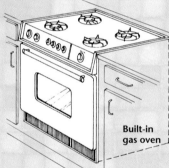

A built-in range is installed in a kitchen cabinet and rests on a wood base or toe-kick. These are particularly useful for a peninsula or island installation. A slide-in range rests on the floor like a freestanding model but is without sides and slides in between two cabinets.

Built-in gas oven

A dual-fuel range has the flexibility of a gas cooktop and the reliability of an electric oven and costs considerably more than a conventional range. It is available in widths from 24 to 48 inches and with a variety of options. Dual-fuel ranges must be installed by a professional; you need a gas line and access to a 220-volt electrical power supply.

A commercial gas range has from four to twelve burners, one or two radiant and/or convection ovens, and sometimes a high shelf or broiler at the top. They perform well, but they are not as well insulated as residential units and are potentially dangerous for young children. Such ranges also require extra support in the floor. So-called residential/commercial units have the look and high-BTU output of commercial units but are better insulated; they also offer features such as self-cleaning ovens.

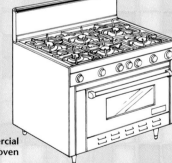

Residential/commercial gas oven

HOODS

A ventilation system consists of a hood to capture the air, an exhaust system to remove it, and a duct to carry the air outside. A hood should cover the entire cooking area and extend 3 to 6 inches on each side; its bottom edge should be 21 to 30 inches above the cooking surface. The power of a fan is rated in cubic feet per minute (CFM), the loudness in sones; a quality hood can handle a minimum of 300 CFM, with a noise level of less than 8 sones. Units with variable-speed controls perform quietly; units with ventilators or blowers installed on the roof or exterior wall are the most quiet.

Installed beneath cabinet

Low-profile

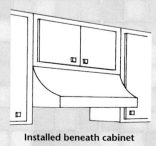

Freestanding

Refrigerators and freezers

A refrigerator or freezer works best when it is two-thirds full, so base your selection on the size of your family, your shopping habits, and your lifestyle. Allow eight to twelve cubic feet for two people, two extra cubic feet for each additional family member, and an extra two cubic feet if you entertain frequently. Allow two cubic feet per person for a freezer compartment.

Refrigerators are 66 to 84 inches high, 24 to 48 inches wide, and 24 to 48 inches deep. If you are placing a new refrigerator in the space of an old one, measure the space carefully and take the measurements with you when you shop. If you are completely remodeling, choose the refrigerator first, then measure for your cabinets around the size of the appliance.

The interior configuration of a refrigerator and how it suits your needs may be more important than its size. Options to consider: adjustable shelves, meat or cheese drawers, crispers with moisture controls, and defrosting capabilities. Other energy-efficient features: separate refrigeration systems for the refrigerator and freezer, energy-saver switches, and a through-the-door shelf to reach foods on an inner shelf without opening the door. An automatic ice maker and water dispenser in the door uses a lot of energy but may be worth it based on your family's needs.

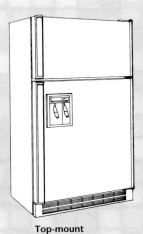

Top-mount

Side-by-side

Top mount. Having the freezer on top, this is the most energy efficient model; it provides easy storage for large items and offers the greatest choices in size and design.

Bottom mount. With the freezer on the bottom, foods in the refrigerator are at eye level. More expensive and less energy efficient than top mounts, and fewer models are available. In-the-door icemakers and water dispensers are not available.

Side-by-side. Refrigerator and freezer next to each other permits easy visibility and access to food, but narrower shelves make storage of bulky items difficult. Wider than the others and takes up more wall space, but the narrow doors need less clearance to open. This style is more costly.

Single door. Smaller and more economical, their lower capacity (10.6 to 13.9 cubic feet) limits the amount of food that can be stored. Freezer compartment has to be defrosted manually and does not stay as cold as a freezer with its own door.

Modular. Undercounter models 33 to 34 inches high with a hinged door or pull-out drawers can be installed in a center island or food prep area.

Built-in. With compressor and condensor units mounted on top, 24-inch-deep built-ins fit into a standard run of cabinets. These models are shallower and use more energy.

Under-counter

FREEZERS

Top-opening chest freezers are less expensive to purchase and operate than uprights. Many require manual defrosting but build up frost more slowly. They take up more floor space but keep foods longer because the temperature remains constant. Measure your space carefully before purchasing. Features include a door lock (absolutely necessary with children), an interior light, a manual-defrost drain, and a safety signal light (in case of a power failure).

Chest

Countertops

Choosing countertop materials is a matter of balancing the look, the practicality, and the cost. Any of the six surfaces below can be installed throughout the kitchen, but consider a combination of materials with different surfaces for different tasks. Also, edge treatments can dress up a counter; look at a bullnose edge, a wood strip, or inlays in a solid surface.

STONE

Granite and marble's cool surfaces are good for working with dough or making candy. Solid stone slabs are very expensive; stone tiles, including slate and limestone, are less expensive alternatives. With stone other than granite, look into the latest sealers.

Pros. Strong and durable, heatproof, water resistant, and easy to clean.

Cons. Heavy and requires a strong base; must be custom installed. Oil, alcohol, and any acid (such as those in lemons or wine) will stain marble or damage its high-gloss finish; granite can stand up to all of these.

PLASTIC LAMINATE

Composed of resin-impregnated paper bonded to a particleboard core, laminate comes in a wide range of colors and textures. Ready-made molded tops called post-formed are the least expensive option.

Pros. Durable, easy to clean, stain and moisture resistant, and relatively inexpensive.

Cons. Can scratch, scorch, and chip. High-gloss surfaces show dirt and water marks. The dark backing shows at the seams.

SOLID SURFACE

Made from polyester or acrylic resins and mineral fillers, this smooth material is manufactured in sheets ½ inch thick that can be formed into seamless designs (with an integral sink, if desired). A variety of edge treatments are possible.

Pros. Durable, water resistant, nonporous, easy to clean, and resists bacteria and mold. Blemishes and scratches can be sanded out.

Cons. Easily scratched, discolored by heat, and expensive. Needs firm support. Usually requires professional installation.

STAINLESS STEEL

Stainless, an alloy of carbon steel that is composed of chromium and nickel, should contain at least 8 to 10 percent nickel and be 18-gauge (thickness). A matte finish is easy on the eyes and easier to clean than a mirror finish.

Pros. Waterproof, heat resistant, easy to clean, durable, and good near water. Available with integrated sinks.

Cons. Can scratch and dent; can't be used for cutting. Fabrication—sink cutouts, faucet holes, and bends and welds for edges and backsplashes—raises the cost. Using flat sheeting with a wood edge reduces the cost.

CERAMIC TILE

Ceramic tile comes in many colors, textures, and patterns. Made of clay that is dried and fired in a kiln, tiles can be glazed or unglazed; nonporous glazed tiles won't soak up spills and stains.

Pros. Installed correctly, it's heatproof, scratch resistant, water resistant, and long lasting. Grout is also available in numerous colors.

Cons. Some glazes react to foods or household chemicals. Grout is hard to keep clean, even when grout sealer is used (using thin grout spaces helps). The hard surface can chip glassware. High-gloss tiles show smudges.

WOOD

Butcher block is strips of edge-grain or end-grain maple or oak that are laminated together. Maple butcher block is sold in 24-, 30-, and 36-inch widths; oak, sugar pine, and birch are also used. Smaller pieces can be used for inserts.

Pros. Handsome, natural, easily installed, easy on glassware and china, reasonably priced, and ideal for a cutting surface.

Cons. Can burn, scratch, and dent, and can't be used near water. Polyurethane, a permanent sealer, can be used on eating but not cutting surfaces.

Flooring

Kitchen floors should be moisture resistant, durable, and easy to clean, as well as aesthetically appealing to you. When making a choice, weigh the physical characteristics of the various flooring materials—resilient, ceramic tile, wood, laminate, and stone—and consider the kind of subflooring you have or will need, as well as the total cost, including the material and installation.

WOOD

The three basic types of wood flooring are strip, narrow tongue-and-groove boards in random lengths; plank, tongue-and-groove boards in various widths and random lengths; and wood tile, often laid in parquet style. For durability, choose only hardwoods, not soft ones like pine or fir. For added durability, finish floors with polyurethane.

Pros. Wood floors are warm, feel good underfoot, resist wear, and can be refinished. They often look better with age.

Cons. Moisture will damage wood floors. An adequate substructure is crucial. Cleaning is an issue: some surfaces can be mopped, some cannot. Polyurethane-finished floors can never be waxed, only buffed. Bleaching and some staining processes may wear unevenly and are difficult to repair.

STONE

Natural stone, such as slate, flagstone, marble, granite, and limestone, is practical when used with sealers and finishes. Stone can be used in its natural shape, called flagstones, with grouted joints or cut into uniform rectangular blocks that are butted together.

Pros. Easy to maintain and virtually indestructible.

Cons. Cold and sometimes slippery underfoot, although new honed or textured surfaces are safer to walk on. It must be sealed, requires a strong, well-supported subfloor, and is costly.

LAMINATE

Similar to laminate countertops, laminate flooring is composed of a layer of veneer with a durable protective coating bonded to a high density fiberboard with a moisture-resistant backing. Available in many looks from wood to stone to solid colors that can look like tile.

Pros. Laminate flooring is durable, easy to install, resistant to dents and stains, and easy to clean.

Cons. Not the best choice near water; if moisture gets under the surface, it can swell. Can sound hollow, unlike solid wood, because it is a floating floor.

RESILIENT

Made of vinyl that comes in square tiles and sheets up to 12 feet wide, eliminating the need for seams in some kitchens. Available in two forms: inlaid, in which color is created with chips fused into the material, and rotogravure, in which the design is printed on the surface. Old-fashioned linoleum and cork are also resilient materials.

Pros. Comfortable to walk on, stain resistant, easy to care for, affordable. A great variety of styles, colors, and textures.

Cons. Vulnerable to dents and scratches, especially in the more economic flooring. Must be installed on a very flat subfloor. "No wax" floors require a manufacturer-recommended floor-care product.

CERAMIC TILE

Floor tiles are thicker and usually larger (at least 8 inches square) than wall tiles. Choices include glazed ceramic tiles (preferably with a matte or textured finish for slip resistance), unglazed terra-cotta pavers, and unglazed quarry tiles that need to be sealed. A good floor choice if you are adding radiant floor heating.

Pros. Very durable and easy to maintain. Available in many sizes and colors.

Cons. Hard on the feet—with no "give"—as well as noisy, cold, and slippery underfoot. Can chip or crack; can be costly. Grouting can be difficult to keep clean and can come loose.

REMODELING BASICS

Any kitchen remodel, no matter how large or small, is an investment in your time and energy. It can also be tedious and full of stress. Here are some survival tips to keep the work going smoothly.

Determine what you want before you begin. A kitchen remodel can be as simple as a new coat of paint on the walls or new undercabinet lighting. A major overhaul can involve moving a wall, installing a dishwasher, or laying a tile floor. Read through this chapter on all aspects of kitchen remodeling for an overview.

Think safety. Keep your family safe during the remodel. Clean up the area every day and dispose of debris carefully. While working, wear protective gear and follow manufacturers' instructions. If you need more detailed information on step-by-step procedures, take a look at the *Sunset* books *Basic Carpentry, Basic Plumbing,* and *Basic Wiring,* or consult a professional.

Think comfort. Whether the job will take one week or several months, you'll need to set up a temporary kitchen with a refrigerator, a surface to work on, and a source of water. Use simple appliances like a toaster oven, hot plate, and microwave.

Communicate. If your family is used to meeting in the kitchen, set up an area of communications to help them feel less dislocated. A bulletin board near a telephone can serve as a message center.

Designate one family member to deal with the contractor or other professionals. If only one person is communicating, mixed messages are less likely to happen.

Lastly, be as flexible as possible, stay focused on the joy of a new kitchen, and keep your sense of humor.

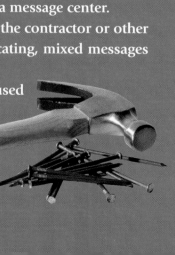

"Be prepared" is the best advice for a kitchen remodel. Before you begin any project, you will want to have a clear idea of the sequence of steps necessary to complete the job, obtain any necessary permits from your local building department, and evaluate your own ability to perform each of the tasks. To do the work yourself, you'll also need the proper materials and tools. After you have a clear understanding of what's involved, you are prepared to begin.

KNOW THYSELF

Be realistic when assessing your do-it-yourself abilities. The level of skill required for a kitchen remodel depends on what improvements you are making. Surface treatments—such as painting, wallpapering, replacing light fixtures, or laying resilient flooring—can be accomplished by a homeowner with just simple do-it-yourself experience. Some projects may require a few specialized tools, usually available from a building supply or home improvement center.

Complex remodeling tasks—such as moving bearing walls, running new drain and vent pipes, or wiring new electrical circuits and service panels—are best handled by professionals. Many smaller jobs in the structural, plumbing, and electrical areas, though, are within the skills of a homeowner with a little experience.

Even if there's not much you can build, you may discover a talent for demolition—and save money in the process; note, however, that some contractors may not want to relinquish this task. If you take it on, be sure you're finished by the time the remodeling crew is ready to begin.

SETTING UP A PLAN

The more involved your remodeling is, the greater the need for careful planning. The following check list will get you off to a good start; be sure to complete it before the work begins.

❑ List the sequence of tasks to be performed, and estimate the time required to complete each one.

❑ If you're hiring professional help, make sure you have firm contracts and schedules with contractors, subcontractors, or other hired workers.

❑ Obtain all required building permits.

❑ Arrange for delivery of materials and make sure you have all the necessary tools on hand.

❑ If electricity, gas, or water must be shut off by the utility company, make sure to arrange for it before work is scheduled to begin.

❑ Find out where you can dispose of refuse, and secure any necessary dumping permits.

❑ Be sure there is a storage area available for temporarily relocating any fixtures or appliances.

❑ Measure fixtures and appliances to make sure there is clearance through doorways and up and down staircases.

HOW TO USE THIS CHAPTER

The sections in this chapter are arranged in the order in which you'd proceed if you were installing an entirely new kitchen. Read consecutively, they'll give you an overview of the scope and sequence of kitchen improvements.

The first three sections survey the relatively complex subjects of structural, plumbing, and electrical systems. Whether or not you plan to do the work yourself, you'd be wise to review these sections for background information. A knowledge of your home's inner workings enables you to plan changes more effectively and to understand the reasons for seemingly arbitrary code restrictions affecting your plans.

Some of your most difficult remodeling hours may be spent tearing out old

work. To minimize the effort, we've included removal procedures within the appropriate installation sections.

If you're planning only one or two simple projects, turn directly to the applicable sections for step-by-step instructions. Special features within the chapter present additional ideas and information for maximum improvement with minimum work and expense.

Steps in Remodeling

This chart will help you plan the sequence of tasks involved in dismantling your old kitchen and installing the new one. Depending on the size of your job and the specific materials you select, you may need to alter the suggested order somewhat. Manufacturers' instructions offer additional guidelines.

Removal sequence

1. Accessories, decorative elements
2. Furniture
3. Contents of cabinets, closets, shelves
4. Fixtures, appliances
5. Countertops, backsplashes
6. Base cabinets, wall cabinets, shelves
7. Floor materials
8. Light fixtures
9. Wallcoverings

Installation sequence

1. Structural changes: walls, doors, windows, skylights
2. Rough plumbing changes
3. Electrical wiring
4. Wall and ceiling coverings
5. Light fixtures
6. Wall cabinets, base cabinets, kitchen islands, shelves
7. Countertops, backsplashes
8. Floor materials
9. Fixtures, appliances
10. Furniture
11. Decorative elements

Acquiring a basic understanding of your kitchen's structural shell is required homework for many kitchen improvements. Your kitchen's framework probably will conform to the pattern of the "typical kitchen," shown in the illustration below.

Starting at the base of the drawing, you'll notice the following framing members: a wooden sill resting on a foundation wall; a series of horizontal, evenly spaced floor joists; and a subfloor (usually plywood sheets) laid atop the joists. This platform supports the first-floor walls, both interior and exterior. The walls are formed by vertical, evenly spaced studs that run between a horizontal sole plate and parallel top plate. The primary wall coverings are fastened directly to the studs.

Depending upon the design of the house, one of several types of construction may be used above the kitchen walls. If there's a second story, a layer of ceiling joists rests on the walls; these joists support both the floor above and the kitchen ceiling below. A one-story house will have either an "open beamed" ceiling—flat or pitched—or a "finished" ceiling. In simple terms, a finished ceiling covers the roof rafters and sheathing which, if exposed, would constitute an open-beamed ceiling. With a flat roof, the finished ceiling is attached directly to the rafters. The ceiling below a pitched roof is attached to joists or to a metal or wooden frame.

REMOVING A PARTITION WALL

Often a major kitchen remodeling means removing all or part of an interior wall to enlarge the space.

Walls that define your kitchen may be bearing or nonbearing. A bearing wall helps support the weight of the house; a nonbearing wall does not. An interior nonbearing wall, often called a partition wall, may be removed without special precautions. The procedure outlined in this section applies to partitions only. If you're considering a remodeling project that involves moving a bearing wall or any wall beneath a second story, consult an architect or contractor about problems and procedures.

How can you tell the difference in walls? All exterior walls running perpendicular to ceiling and floor joists are bearing. Normally, at least one main interior wall is also a bearing wall. If possible, climb up into the attic or crawlspace and check the ceiling joists. If they are joined over any wall, that wall is bearing. Even if joists span the entire width of the house, their midsections may be resting on a bearing wall at the point of maximum allowable span. If you have any doubts about the wall, consult an architect, contractor, or building inspector.

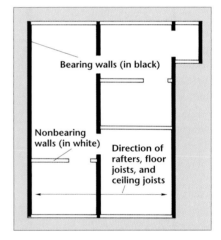

Bearing walls (in black)

Nonbearing walls (in white)

Direction of rafters, floor joists, and ceiling joists

Though removing a partition wall is not complicated, it can be quite messy. Cover the floors and furnishings, and wear a dust mask, safety glasses, and gloves. Ensure adequate ventilation. NOTE: Check the wall for signs of electrical wiring, water and drainpipes, or heating and ventilation ducts. Any of these obstructions must be carefully rerouted before you remove the wall.

Removing the wallcovering. If there's a door in the wall, remove it from its hinges. Pry off any door trim, ceiling molding, and base molding.

The most common wallcovering is drywall (or gypsum wallboard) nailed to wall studs. To remove it, knock holes

BASIC STRUCTURAL ANATOMY

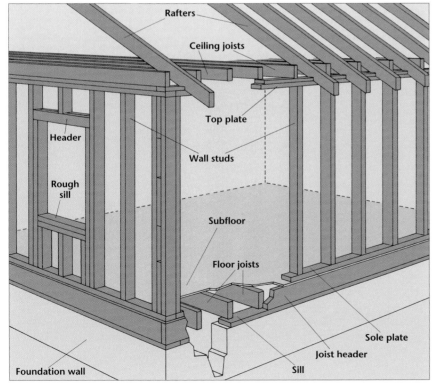

Rafters

Ceiling joists

Top plate

Header

Wall studs

Rough sill

Subfloor

Floor joists

Sole plate

Joist header

Foundation wall

Sill

HOW TO REMOVE WALL FRAMING

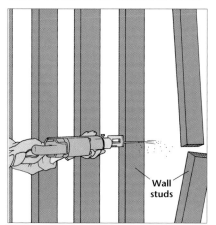

Saw through the middle of the wall studs; bend the studs sideways to free the nails from the top and sole plates.

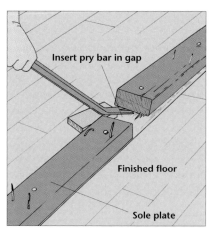

Cut gaps through the sole plate with a saw and chisel; insert a pry bar in each side of the gap to free the sole plate.

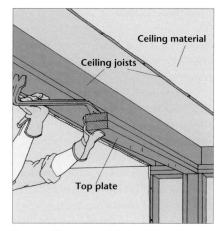

Strip ceiling materials back from the top plate, cut gaps in the plate, and pry out sections of the plate.

in the drywall with a hammer, then pull it away from the studs with a pry bar. After one side is removed, hit the other side from behind to knock it free.

If the wall covering is plaster and lath, chisel away the plaster until the lath backing—wood strips or metal—is exposed. You'll have to cut through the lath to break it up; then pry the lath and plaster away from the studs.

Dismantling the framing. Remove studs by sawing through the middle of each one; then push and pull them sideways to free the nails. To get at end studs (attached to studs or nailing blocks in adjacent walls), first strip wallcoverings back to the bordering studs; then saw and pry as required.

To remove the sole plate, saw a small section out of the middle down to the finished floor level, chisel through the remaining thickness, and insert a pry bar in the gap.

To remove a top plate that lies parallel to the joists, cut ceiling materials back to adjacent joists and pry off the plate. If the top plate is perpendicular to the joists, cut an even 2-foot strip in the ceiling materials, making certain that you don't cut into joists; remove the plate.

Patching walls, ceilings, and floors. Drywall and plaster aren't difficult to patch; the real challenge lies in matching a special texture, wallpaper, shade

of paint, or well-aged floor. This is not a problem if your remodeling plans call for new wall coverings, ceiling, or flooring. In either case, see the sections "Walls and ceilings" (pages 86–91) and "Flooring" (pages 98–103) for techniques and tips.

FRAMING A NEW WALL

To separate a kitchen from an adjoining living area or to subdivide space within the kitchen, you may need to build a new partition wall.

Framing a wall is a straightforward task, but you must measure carefully and continue to check the alignment as work progresses. The basic steps are listed below. To install a doorway, see page 70.

Plotting the location. The new wall must be anchored securely to the floor, ceiling joists, and, if possible, to wall framing on one side.

To locate the studs, try knocking with your fist along the wall until the

WALL FRAMING COMPONENTS

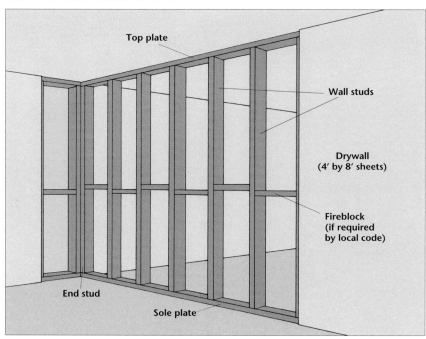

sound changes from hollow to solid. If you have drywall, you can use an inexpensive stud finder; often, though, the nails that hold drywall to the studs are visible on close inspection. Stud finders do not work with plaster walls. You may have to drill a series of small holes to locate the studs.

To locate ceiling joists, use the same methods or, from the attic or crawlspace, drive small nails down through the ceiling on both sides of a joist to serve as reference points below. Adjacent joists and studs should be evenly spaced, usually 16 or 24 inches away from those you've located.

A wall running perpendicular to the joists will demand the least effort to attach. If wall and joists will run parallel, though, try to center the wall under a single joist; otherwise, you'll need to install nailing blocks every 2 feet between two parallel joists (see illustration above right). If the side of the new wall falls between existing studs, you'll need to install additional nailing blocks.

On the ceiling, mark both ends of the center line of the new wall. Now measure 1¾ inches (half the width of a 2 by 4 top plate) on both sides of each mark; snap parallel lines between corresponding marks with a chalkline; the top plate will occupy the space between the lines.

Positioning the sole plate. Hang a plumb bob from each end of the lines you just marked and mark these new points on the floor. Snap two more chalklines to connect the floor points.

Cut both sole plate and top plate

HOW TO ANCHOR A TOP PLATE

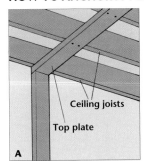
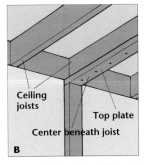
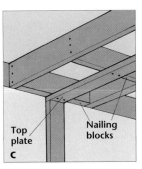

To anchor a top plate, nail to perpendicular joists (A), to the bottom of the parallel joist (B), or install nailing blocks between the parallel joists (C).

to the desired length. Lay the sole plate between the lines on the floor and nail it in place with 10-penny nails spaced every 2 feet. (If you have a masonry floor, use a masonry bit to drill holes through the sole plate every 2 or 3 feet. Then insert expansion bolts.)

If you're planning a doorway (see "Framing a doorway," page 70), don't nail through that section of the plate; it will be cut out later.

Marking stud positions. Lay the top plate against the sole plate, as shown in the illustration below. Beginning at the end that will be attached to an existing stud or to nailing blocks, measure in 1½ inches—the thickness of a 2 by 4 stud—and draw a line across both plates with a combination square. Starting once more from that end, measure and draw lines at 15¼ and 16¾ inches at a time, drawing new lines, until the far end of both plates is reached. Each set of lines will outline the placement of a stud, with all studs evenly spaced 16 inches

"on center" (O.C.). Don't worry if the spacing at the far end is less than 16 inches. (If local codes permit, consider 24-inch spacing—you'll save lumber—and adjust the initial placement of lines to 23¼ and 24¾ inches.)

Fastening the top plate. With two helpers, lift the top plate into position between the lines (marked on the ceiling); nail it to perpendicular joists, to one parallel joist, or to nailing blocks, as shown above.

Attaching the studs. Measure and cut the studs to exact length. Attach one end stud (or both) to existing studs or to nailing blocks between studs. Lift the remaining studs into place one at a time; line them up on the marks, and check for plumb with a carpenter's level. Toenail the studs to both top plate and sole plate with 8-penny nails.

Many building codes require horizontal fireblocks between studs. The number of rows depends on the code; if permitted, position blocks to provide an extra nailing surface for wall materials.

Finishing. After the studs are installed, add electrical outlets and switches (see pages 80–82), as well as new plumbing (see pages 74–76). It's also time for the building inspector to check your work. Following the inspection, you can apply your wall-coverings (see pages 86–91), patch the ceiling, and add base moldings.

HOW TO MARK STUD POSITIONS

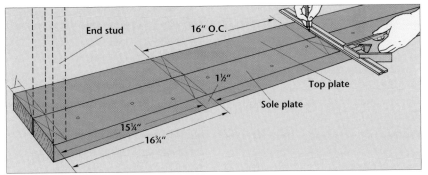

HOW TO FRAME A DOORWAY

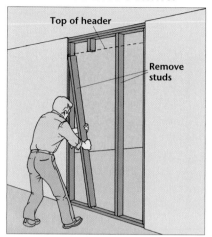

Mark and cut studs within the opening, even with the top of the new header.

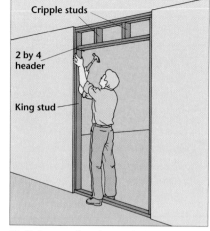

Nail the new header to the king studs; nail into ends of the new cripple studs.

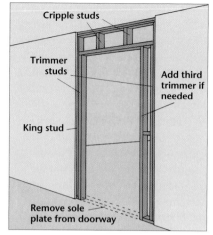

Nail trimmer studs to the king studs; block out a third trimmer if needed.

FRAMING A DOORWAY

Relocating kitchen cabinets, counters, or appliances or simply redirecting traffic flow may involve moving a door opening. Covering an existing door is relatively easy (see below). To create a new opening, it's necessary to remove wall materials, add door framing, and possibly hang a new door. Be sure the wall you plan to cut into is a nonbearing wall (see "Removing a partition wall," page 67). If the wall contains electrical wires, pipes, or ductwork, they must be rerouted.

Positioning the opening. Are you planning an open doorway, or a frame for a bifold, sliding, or standard prehung door? Determine the door type before starting work, and check the manufacturer's "rough opening" dimensions—that is the exact wall opening required after the new framing is in place.

You'll need to plan an opening large enough to accommodate both the rough opening and the rough door framing—an additional 1½ inches on top and sides. If you're recycling an old door or your new unit did not come with rough opening dimensions, add an additional ⅜ inch on all sides for shimming (adjusting level and plumb) the typical door frame.

Often it's simpler to remove the drywall from floor to ceiling between two bordering studs (the new king

studs) that will remain in place. (This is the method illustrated.) In any case, you'll save work later if you can use at least one existing stud as part of the rough framing.

Regardless of the method you choose, use a carpenter's level for a straightedge, and mark the outline of the opening on the wall.

Removing wall covering and studs. First remove any base molding. Cut along the door outline with a circular saw cut to the depth of the wall covering only, being careful to sever only the drywall, not the studs beneath. Pry the drywall away from the framing. To remove plaster and lath, chisel through the plaster to expose the lath, then cut the lath and pry it loose.

Cut the studs inside the opening to the height required for the header (see drawing above). Using a combination square, mark these studs on the face and one side, then cut carefully with a reciprocating or keyhole saw. Pry the cut studs loose from the sole plate.

Framing the opening. With wall covering and studs removed, you're ready to frame the opening. Measure and cut the header (for a partition wall you can use a 2 by 4 laid flat), and toenail it to the king studs with 8-penny nails. Nail the header

to the bottoms of the cripple studs.

Cut the sole plate within the opening, and pry it away from the subfloor.

Cut trimmer studs and nail them to the king studs with 10-penny nails in a staggered pattern. You'll probably need to adjust the width by blocking out a third trimmer from one side, as shown above right.

Hanging the door. Bifold, swinging, or sliding pocket doors are commonly used in kitchens. Methods of hanging doors vary considerably, depending on type. Check the manufacturer's instructions carefully before you plan the wall opening.

Even if you're not hanging a door, you'll probably want to install a pre-assembled door frame—consisting of a top jamb and two side jambs—to cover the rough framing.

Installing trim. When the framing is completed and the door is hung, you can patch the drywall and install new trim (casing) around the opening. Some prehung doors have casing attached.

CLOSING A DOORWAY

It's easy to eliminate an existing doorway. Simply add new studs within the opening and attach new wallcoverings. The only trick is to match the present wall surface.

First, remove the casing around the opening. Then remove the door from its hinges or guide track and pry any jambs or tracks away from the rough framing.

Next, measure the gap on the floor between the existing trimmer studs; cut a length of 2 by 4 to serve as a new sole plate. Nail it to the floor with 10-penny nails. (If you have a masonry floor, attach the 2 by 4 with expansion bolts.)

Measure and cut new 2 by 4 studs to fill the space; position studs at 16-inch intervals on center. Toenail the studs to the new sole plate and the header with 8-penny nails. Add fireblocks between studs if required by the local code.

Strip the wall coverings back far enough to give yourself a firm nailing surface and an even edge. Then add new coverings to match the existing ones (see pages 86–87), or resurface the entire wall. Match or replace the baseboard molding.

WINDOW BASICS

Framing and hanging a window is similar to installing a door (see page 70), though in addition you must cut into the exterior siding and sheathing of the house. But the most important factor to consider is the possibility that you may be dealing with a bearing wall (see page 67). Removing studs from a bearing wall means constructing a temporary support wall before you start work and using more rigid framing than that required for partition wall openings.

An outline of basic installation follows. For details about tools and help with step-by-step techniques, consult the manufacturer's instructions or your window dealer.

Removing an existing window. First remove any interior and exterior trim that's not an integral part of the unit. Take out the sash, if possible (see drawing above); then remove the frame. The window may have been nailed directly to the rough framing materials or may have been secured by flanges or brackets.

BASIC WINDOW COMPONENTS

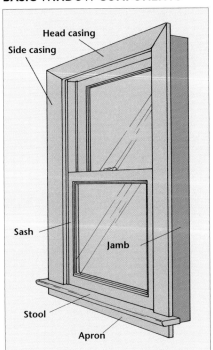

Head casing
Side casing
Sash
Stool
Apron
Jamb

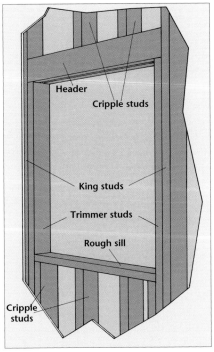

Header
Cripple studs
King studs
Trimmer studs
Rough sill
Cripple studs

Basic window framing. Unlike rough door framing, window framing includes cripple studs at the top and bottom. The rough sill—a length of 2 by 4 or 2 by 6 lumber laid flat and sometimes doubled for strength—lies at the bottom edge of the opening. The top edge is bounded by the header. The header for a bearing wall opening and (depending on local codes) for any exterior wall is typically composed of matching lengths of "2 by" framing lumber turned on edge, with ½-inch-thick plywood spacers sandwiched between them. The exact size of 2-by material required depends on both the width of the window opening and your local building code.

Cutting a new opening. You should receive a rough opening size for your new window from the manufacturer. (If not, measure the unit and add an extra ⅜ inch on all sides for leveling and plumbing the window.) The actual opening will be somewhat larger; add to the rough opening size the dimensions of the king studs, trimmer studs, header, and sill. Work from the inside of the house outward. If possible, complete the rough framing before opening the exterior.

Installing a prehung window. A prehung window arrives with the sash already installed inside the window frame—and frequently with the exterior casing (trim) attached. To simply replace an existing window with another of the same size, first remove the interior trim and measure the rough opening; then order the new window to fit.

Using wood shims or blocks, center, level, and plumb the new window in the opening; then fasten it to the rough framing. Depending on the window type, you will either nail through a flange into the outside sheathing, screw the jambs to the header and trimmer studs, or nail through preassembled exterior trim.

Finishing touches. Your new window may need exterior casing and a drip cap. Or you may be required to install metal flashing over the unit's top edge. In any event, be sure to caulk the joints thoroughly between the siding and the new window.

Cover the top and sides of the inside opening with casing and install a finished stool over the rough sill. Finally, add one last strip of casing (called an apron).

Choosing windows

Windows let in natural light, which makes a kitchen not only warmer and friendlier but also a safer place in which to work. In choosing new windows, there are several factors to keep in mind.

WINDOW FRAMES

The choice of the window frame material will determine its look as well as the amount of maintenance required.

Wood-framed windows are traditional and can be painted or stained. Wood is a relatively good insulator.

Aluminum-framed windows are less expensive than wood and need less maintenance.

Cladding is a protective coating made of aluminum or vinyl that needs little maintenance and is moderately priced.

GLAZING

Glazing is the term that refers both to the glass installed in a window or door and to the act of installing the glass.

Single glazing is one sheet of glass. Double glazing is two panes of glass sealed with a space between the panes. An inert gas such as argon or krypton fills the space in insulating windows.

Triple glazing is the use of three panes of glass enclosing two separate air spaces.

Low-E glass is a term that refers to the low emissivity of glass, its ability to block ultraviolet rays from the sun and to restrict the flow of heat. Low-E glass has a metallic coating on the glass or a film suspended between the two layers.

R-VALUE AND U-VALUE

R-value and U-value are terms developed by the U.S. Department of Energy and used by the building industry to rate windows and building materials.

R-value is the measure of the resistance a material has to heat flow.

The higher the number, the greater the material's insulating capability.

U-value or U-factor is a measure of heat flow through a window or wall.

The lower the U-factor, the better the material's insulating capability.

WINDOW STYLES

Double-hung

A double-hung window has two sashes that slide up and down to open. Older windows use weights and a rope or chain, newer models coiled springs, to keep the windows open.

Casement

A casement is a hinged window that is operated by a crank or lever. These windows swing out to open either to the right or left.

Awning

An awning window is hinged on the top and opened with a crank. Often used in basements or under eaves, awning windows can also be combined with other windows.

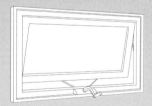

Jalousie

Jalousie windows, made of glass panes that are opened and closed by a system of pivots and levers driven by a crank, are used mostly in warm climates, because they do not seal completely.

Bay

A bay window is a set of windows that protrude out from the wall, forming an angular alcove. The center window is the largest and usually a fixed window. The two side windows can open or be fixed.

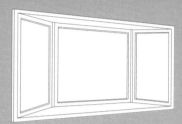

Bow

A bow window is similar to a bay window except it is curved rather than angular. It is made of four or more units.

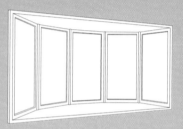

Sliding

In a sliding window, also called a gliding window, the sashes slide sideways to open and close. In some models one sash is fixed and the other slides.

Fixed

A fixed window is a stationary window, one that does not open. It can be a large rectangular picture window or a small window in one of a variety of shapes.

SKYLIGHT BASICS

Installing a skylight in a pitched roof with asphalt or wood shingles is a two-part process: you cut and frame openings in both roof and ceiling, and connect the two openings with a vertical or angled light shaft. (You don't need a light shaft for a flat roof or an open-beamed ceiling, which requires only a single opening.) Here is a brief description of the installation sequence; for complete information on the tools and techniques required for the job, consult the manufacturer's instructions or your skylight dealer.

Marking the openings. Using the rough opening measurements supplied by the manufacturer, mark the location of the ceiling opening; then drive nails up through the four corners and center so they'll be visible in the attic or crawlspace. From the attic, check for obstructions, shifting the location if necessary. You'll save work if you can use one or two ceiling joists as the edges of your opening.

With a plumb bob, transfer the ceiling marks to the underside of the roof; again, drive nails up through the roofing materials to mark the location. If you run into obstructions on the roof, change the position slightly and use an angled light shaft to connect the two openings.

Framing the roof opening. On a day with zero probability of rain, cut and frame the roof opening. Exercise extreme caution when working on the roof; if the pitch is steep or if you have a tile or slate roof, you should strongly consider leaving this part to professionals.

When you work with a skylight designed to be mounted on a curb frame, build the curb first; 2 by 6 lumber is commonly used. (If your skylight has an integral curb or is self-flashing, you do not need to build a curb.)

To determine the actual size of the opening you need to cut, add the dimensions of any framing materials (see below) to the rough opening size marked by the nails. You may need to

BASIC SKYLIGHT COMPONENTS

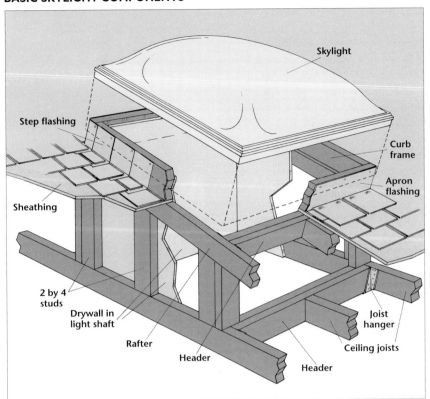

remove some extra shingles or roofing materials down to the sheathing to accommodate the flashing of a curb-mounted unit or the flange of a self-flashing unit.

Cut the roof opening in successive layers as follows: roofing materials first; sheathing next, and finally any necessary rafters. Before cutting the rafters, support them by 2 by 4s nailed to the ceiling joists below.

To frame the opening, you'll need double headers and possibly trimmers. You will want to install the headers with double joist hangers.

If you're installing a curb-mounted unit, position and flash the curb. Toe-nail the curb to the rafters or trimmers and to the headers. Pay special attention to the manufacturer's instructions concerning directions for flashing.

Mounting the skylight. For a curb-mounted unit, secure the skylight to the top of the curb with nails and a sealant. Set a self-flashing unit in roofing cement, then nail through the flange directly into the roof sheathing. Coat the joints and nail holes with more roofing cement.

Opening the ceiling. Double-check your original ceiling marks against the roof opening and the intended angle of the light shaft. Cut through the ceiling materials and then sever the joists. Support joists to be cut by bracing them against adjacent joists. Frame the ceiling opening in the same manner you used for the roof opening.

Building a light shaft. Measure the distance between the ceiling headers and roof headers at each corner and at 16-inch intervals between the corners. Cut studs to fit these measurements and install them as illustrated above. Nail or screw the drywall to the framing.

Final touches. Insulate the spaces between studs in the light shaft before fastening wallcoverings to the studs. Painting drywall white maximizes reflected light.

Trim the ceiling openings as required. Adding a plastic ceiling panel (one that's either manufactured or cut to size) helps diffuse light evenly.

Do you know how your plumbing system works? If not, the kitchen is a good place to start learning, for the plumbing here is much less complicated than in other areas—bathrooms, for instance.

A PLUMBING OVERVIEW

Three complementary sets of pipes work together to fill your home's plumbing needs: the drain-waste and vent (DWV) systems, and the water supply system. In the typical kitchen, these pipes serve the "sink complex"—the sink and related appliances, such as the dishwasher and garbage disposer.

The supply system. Water that eventually arrives at your kitchen faucet enters the house from the public water main or from a source on the property. At the water service entrance, the main supply line divides in two—one line branching off to be heated by the water heater, the other remaining as cold water. The two pipes usually run parallel below the first-floor level until they reach the vicinity of a group of fixtures, then head up through the wall or floor. Sometimes the water supply—hot, cold, or both—passes through a water softener or filter (see drawing below) before reaching the fixtures.

Drain-waste and vent systems. The drain-waste pipes channel waste water and solid wastes to the sewer line. Vent pipes carry away sewer gas and maintain atmospheric pressure in drainpipes and fixture traps.

Every house has a main soil stack that serves a dual function: below the level of the fixtures it is your home's primary drainpipe; at its upper end, which protrudes through the roof, the stack becomes a vent. Drainpipes from individual fixtures, as well as larger branch drains, connect to the main stack. A fixture or fixture group located on a branch drain far from the main stack will have a secondary vent stack of its own rising to the roof.

The sink complex. Generally, a single set of vertical supply pipes and one drainpipe serve the entire kitchen. For both convenience and economy, fixtures and appliances that require water usually are adjacent to the sink. Supply pipes for a dishwasher, hot water dispenser, and automatic ice maker branch off the main hot and cold supply lines leading to the sink faucet. Similarly, the dishwasher and disposer share the sink's trap and drainpipe. The hot water dispenser discharges directly into the sink.

ROUGHING IN NEW PLUMBING

You will need to add new plumbing to your kitchen if you move your present sink and related appliances, plumb a

A PLUMBING OVERVIEW

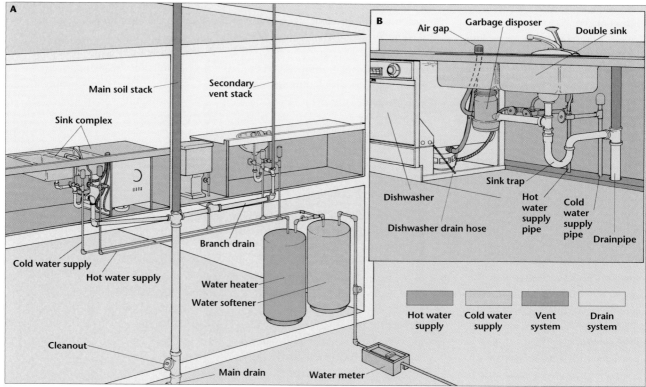

Your kitchen's plumbing is part of a coordinated system of hot and cold supply pipes leading water to fixtures and appliances, and drain-waste and vent pipes carrying wastes and gases away (A). Kitchen plumbing is commonly concentrated in the "sink complex" area (B).

sink into a new kitchen island, or add a new fixture—such as a second sink.

If you have pipefitting experience from previous plumbing projects, you may be able to handle these jobs yourself. But if you're not confident of your abilities, consider hiring a professional plumber to rough in the new pipes. When that work is finished, you can then hook up the fixtures or appliances yourself; refer to pages 104–111.

Mapping your present system. If you're considering a plumbing change or addition, you'll first need a detailed map of your home's present plumbing. Begin your investigation from an unfinished basement or crawlspace or, if necessary, from the attic or roof. Locate the main stack, branch drains, and any secondary stacks. Positioning yourself directly below or above the kitchen, try to determine whether the sink complex is tied directly into the main stack or connected to a branch drain with its own vent. Find the spot where vertical supply lines branch off from horizontal lines and head up into a wall or the floor.

Extending DWV pipes. Your plans to relocate a sink or add a new fixture depend on the feasibility of extending present DWV pipes. This in turn is often determined by local regulations. Plumbing codes, both national and local, are quite specific about the size

of the drainpipe or branch drain serving the kitchen sink complex or any new fixture requiring drainage; the distance (called the "critical distance") from the traps to the main stack, secondary stack, or other vent; and the point where a new drainpipe or branch drain ties into the branch drain or main stack.

A proposed fixture located within a few feet of the main stack (check local codes for the exact distance) usually can be drained and vented directly by the stack. New fixtures distant from the stack probably will require a new branch drain beneath the floor, running either to the stack or to an existing cleanout in the main drain (see the drawing below); you'll also need to run a new secondary stack up to the roof.

The drainpipe required for a kitchen sink complex normally has a diameter of at least 1½ inches (2 inches if you plan to vent directly into the stack). Minimum vent size for a secondary stack is commonly 1¼ inches, unless a dishwasher installed without a separate air gap necessitates a larger pipe.

Older DWV pipes probably are made of cast iron, with "hub" or "bell and spigot" ends joined by molten lead and oakum. To extend the system, you may substitute "hubless" or "no-hub" fittings (consisting of neoprene gaskets and stainless steel clamps), which are simpler to install.

Since plastic is lighter than cast iron and is easily joined with solvent cement, you may want to use ABS (acrylonitrile-butadiene-styrene) or PVC (polyvinyl chloride) pipe in your extension. First check the local code; some areas restrict or prohibit the use of plastic pipe.

Extending supply pipes. Because no venting is required, extending supply pipes is a much easier task than extending the DWV system. The selection of

PIPES AND FITTINGS

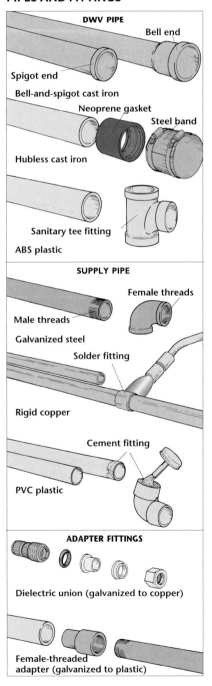

DWV PIPE

Bell end

Spigot end

Bell-and-spigot cast iron

Neoprene gasket

Steel band

Hubless cast iron

Sanitary tee fitting

ABS plastic

SUPPLY PIPE

Female threads

Male threads

Galvanized steel

Solder fitting

Rigid copper

Cement fitting

PVC plastic

ADAPTER FITTINGS

Dielectric union (galvanized to copper)

Female-threaded adapter (galvanized to plastic)

HOW TO EXTEND YOUR PLUMBING SYSTEM

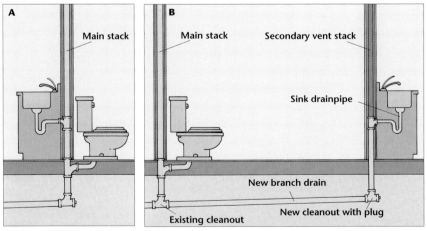

A — Main stack

B — Main stack — Secondary vent stack

Sink drainpipe

New branch drain

Existing cleanout

New cleanout with plug

To drain kitchen plumbing additions, you can either (A) tap into the present main stack, if nearby, or (B) install a new branch drain and secondary vent stack.

correctly sized pipes, as outlined in detail by local codes, depends equally on the type of fixture to be added, the volume of water it demands, and the length of the new pipe.

Your home's supply pipes most likely are either galvanized steel (referred to as "galvanized" or "iron" pipe) connected by threaded fittings, or rigid copper joined with soldered fittings. Some local codes permit the use of plastic supply lines; special adapters will enable you to convert from one material to another (see page 75).

Routing new pipes. Ideally, new drainpipes should be routed below the kitchen floor. They can be suspended from floor joists by pipe hangers (A), inserted in the space between parallel studs (B), or threaded through notches or holes drilled in perpendicular joists (C). The last two methods tend to weaken joists, so should be used with caution. If you have a finished basement, you'll need to cut into the ceiling to thread pipes between or through joists, hide the pipes with a dropped ceiling, or box them in. Drainpipes must slope away from fixtures; a minimum slope of ¼ inch per foot is usually required.

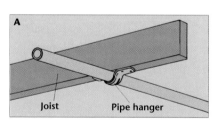

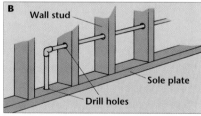

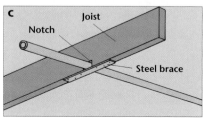

A new vent stack must be installed inside an existing wall (a big job), built into a new or "thickened" wall (see "Building a wet wall," below), or concealed in a closet or cabinet. In mild climates, an enclosed vent may also run up the exterior of the house, within a box.

Supply pipes normally follow drainpipes, but for convenience can be routed directly up through the wall or floor from main horizontal lines below. Supply pipes should run parallel to each other, at least 6 inches apart.

Building a wet wall. The main soil stack, and often a secondary stack, are commonly hidden inside an oversized house wall called a "wet wall."

Unlike an ordinary 2 by 4 stud wall (shown on page 68), a wet wall has a sole plate and top plate built from 2 by 6 or 2 by 8 lumber. Additionally, the 2 by 4 studs are set in pairs, on edge, as shown below. This construction creates maximum space inside the wall for large DWV pipes, which often are wider than a standard wall, and for the fittings, which are wider yet.

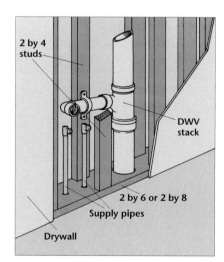

You can also "fur out" an existing wall to hide added pipes—attach new 2 by 4s to the old ones, then add new wallcoverings (see above right). Similarly, a new branch drain that can't run below the floor may be hidden by furring strips laid beside the pipe and covered with new flooring materials. (For flooring details, see pages 98–103.)

GAS SYSTEM BASICS

When you convert from electricity to gas or when you want to relocate a gas appliance, keep in mind a few basic guidelines.

Materials approved for gas supply vary with the area and the type of gas. The most universally accepted materials are threaded pipe of galvanized steel, and "black pipe" (steel pipe without galvanizing). Heavier grades of copper pipe used for plumbing systems (types K and L) are also permitted in some locations.

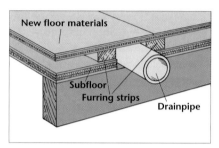

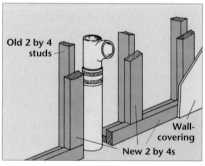

The local plumbing code, or a separate gas code, will specify pipe size according to cubic foot capacity and the length of pipe between the meter or storage tank and the appliance. All gas appliances should have a numerical rating in BTUs per hour stamped right on the nameplate. To convert BTUs to cubic feet, figure 1,000 BTUs to 1 cubic foot; for example, 65,000 BTUs equals 65 cubic feet.

Each appliance must have a nearby code-approved shutoff valve with a straight handle, to turn off the gas in an emergency.

There's no room for error when installing a gas system. It's advisable to have a professional make the installation. You must, in any case, have the work inspected and tested before the gas is turned on.

What may appear to be a hopelessly tangled maze of wires running through the walls and ceiling of your home is actually a well-organized system of circuits. In your kitchen, those circuits serve the light fixtures, switches, and power outlets. Some circuits run directly to large appliances.

In this section you'll find an explanation of your home's electrical system as it relates to kitchen lighting and appliances. Outlined here are the techniques necessary to make basic electrical improvements. If you're replacing your light fixtures or adding new ones, refer to pages 83–85 for help in installing them.

Should you do your own electrical work? It's not always permitted. Local building departments restrict the extent and type of new wiring a homeowner may undertake. In some areas, for example, you may not be permitted to add a new circuit to the service panel. Or if the wiring inside the walls of an older home is the knob-and-tube variety, local regulations may require that new hookups be made by licensed electricians. When restrictions don't apply, problems can still crop up. If you have any doubt about how to proceed, it's always best to hire a professional.

However, if you choose to do any of the work yourself, talk with your building department's electrical inspector about local codes, the National Electrical Code (NEC), and your area's requirements concerning permits and inspections.

UNDERSTANDING YOUR SYSTEM

Today most homes have what's called "three wire" service. The utility company connects three wires to your service entrance panel. Each of two "hot" wires supplies electricity at approximately 120 volts. During normal operation, the third—or "neutral"—wire is maintained at zero volts. Don't be misled, though, by the harmless sound of "neutral"; all three wires are "live."

Three-wire service provides both 120-volt and 240-volt capabilities. One hot wire and the neutral wire combine to supply 120 volts, used for most household appliances. Both hot wires and the neutral wire can complete a 120/240-volt circuit for such needs as an electric range or clothes dryer.

Many older homes have only two-wire service, with one hot wire at 120 volts and one neutral wire. Two-wire service does not have 240-volt capability.

Service entrance panel. This panel is the control center for your electrical system. Inside you'll find the main disconnect (main fuses or main circuit breaker), the fuses or circuit breakers protecting individual circuits, and the grounding connection for the entire system.

After entering the panel and passing through the main disconnect, each hot wire connects to one of two "bus bars," as shown below. These bars accept the amount of current permitted by the main disconnect and allow you to divide that current into smaller branch circuits. The neutral wire is attached to a neutral bus bar, which is in direct contact with the earth through the grounding electrode conductor.

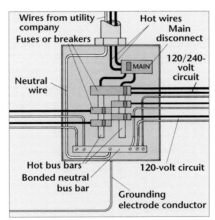

Your home may also have one or more subpanels from which branch circuits originate. A subpanel is an extension of the service entrance panel; the two are connected by hot and neutral "subfeeds."

Simple circuitry. The word "circuit" represents the course that electric current travels; carried by the hot wire, it passes from the service entrance panel or subpanel to one or more devices using electricity (such as a group of light fixtures), then returns to the panel by way of the neutral wire. The devices are normally connected by parallel wiring, as shown below. The hot and neutral wires run continuously from one fixture or outlet box to another; separate wires branch off to individual devices.

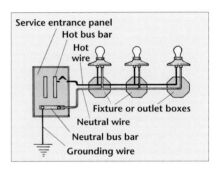

Each 120-volt circuit consists of one hot wire and one neutral wire. The hot wire originates at a branch circuit fuse or circuit breaker connected to one of the hot bus bars. A 120/240-volt circuit, which requires both hot wires, is connected through the fuse or breaker to both hot bus bars. All neutral conductors originate at the neutral bus bar inside the panel.

Grounding prevents shock. The NEC requires that every circuit have a grounding system. Grounding ensures that all metal parts of a wiring system will be maintained at zero volts. In the event of a short circuit, a grounding wire carries current back to the service entrance panel and ensures that the fuse or circuit breaker opens, shutting off the flow of electric current.

The grounding wire for each circuit is attached to the neutral bus bar and then is run with the hot and neutral wires; individual "jumper" wires branch off to ground individual metal devices and boxes as required.

PLANNING ELECTRICAL IMPROVEMENTS

Before you start daydreaming about new track lighting, a dishwasher, or a disposer, you'll need to know whether your present system can handle the additional load.

Service type and rating. First, determine your present type of electrical service. Looking through the window of your meter, you'll see several numbers on the faceplate: 120V indicates two-wire service; 240V indicates three-wire service that provides both 120-volt and 240-volt capabilities.

Your electrical system is also rated for the maximum amount of current (measured in amperes, or "amps") it can carry. This "service rating," determined by the size of the service entrance equipment, should be stamped on the main fuses or circuit breaker. If your system doesn't have a main disconnect, call your utility company or building department for the rating.

Codes. Requirements for electrical circuits serving a modern kitchen and dining area are clearly prescribed by the NEC. Plug-in outlets and switches for small appliances and the refrigerator must be served by a minimum of two 20-amp circuits. Light fixtures are not connected to these circuits, but they share one or more 15-amp circuits. Any outlet on the countertop should be protected with a ground-fault circuit interrupter (GFCI).

If you're installing a dishwasher and/or disposer, you'll need a separate 20-amp circuit for each. Most electric ranges use an individual 50-amp, 120/240-volt major appliance circuit. Wall ovens and a separate cooktop may share a 50-amp circuit.

Tapping into a present circuit. A circuit can be tapped wherever there's an accessible housing box (see "Selecting a power source," page 79). Because of code restrictions, though, you must tap the correct type of circuit.

It's also very important to determine that the circuit you're planning to tap doesn't already carry the maximum load allowed. For help in mapping your circuits, consult an electrician or your local building department.

Adding a new circuit. When an existing circuit can't handle a new load or when a new appliance requires its own circuit, you can often add a new circuit or a subpanel. However, your present house load combined with the proposed addition still must not exceed your service rating.

To help calculate the house load, the NEC has established representative values and formulas based on typical electrical usage. For further aid check with your building department's electrical inspector.

Older homes with two-wire service of less than 100 amps simply can't support many major improvements. If you want to add a new oven or dishwasher you may need to increase your service type and rating, which means replacing the service entrance equipment.

WORKING WITH WIRE

To wire basic extensions to your present electrical circuits, you'll need a few tools and materials, a knack for making wire splices, and the patience to route new wire from box to box and then patch the wall and ceiling materials. For work on this scale,

TYPICAL KITCHEN CIRCUITS

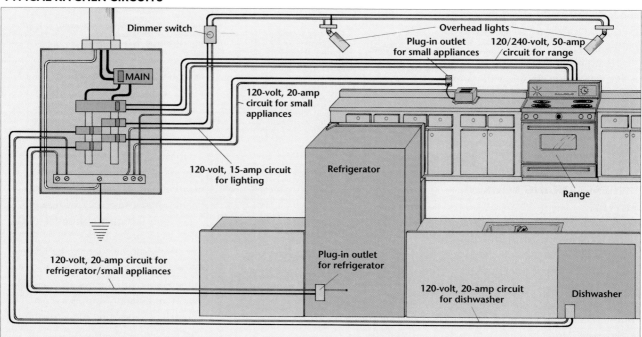

Dimmer switch

Overhead lights

Plug-in outlet for small appliances

120/240-volt, 50-amp circuit for range

MAIN

120-volt, 20-amp circuit for small appliances

120-volt, 15-amp circuit for lighting

Refrigerator

Range

120-volt, 20-amp circuit for refrigerator/small appliances

Plug-in outlet for refrigerator

120-volt, 20-amp circuit for dishwasher

Dishwasher

check about getting an electrical permit; it will probably be required.

Here's the most important rule for all do-it-yourself electricians: NEVER WORK ON ANY "LIVE" CIRCUIT, FIXTURE, PLUG-IN OUTLET, OR SWITCH. YOUR LIFE MAY DEPEND ON IT.

Before starting to work, you must disconnect the circuit at its source, either in the service entrance panel or in a separate subpanel. If fuses protect your circuits, remove the appropriate fuse. In a panel or subpanel equipped with circuit breakers, switch the breakers to the OFF position to disconnect the circuit, then tape down the switch for extra safety.

Selecting a power source.
A circuit can be extended from a present outlet box, fixture box, switch box, or junction box. The one exception is a switch box without a neutral wire (see page 82).

Before deciding which box to tap, consider how you'll route wire to the new switch, outlet, or fixture. Look for the easiest paths behind walls, above ceilings, and under floors. Then choose the most convenient power source.

The box tapped must be large enough to accommodate the new wires (minimum box sizes are specified by the NEC) and must have a knockout hole through which you can thread the cable. If your box doesn't meet these requirements, you must replace it with one that does.

Preparing for new boxes.
Housing boxes—capped with fixture canopies, outlet plates, or switch plates—come in many shapes and sizes. For outlets,

switches, and fixtures weighing 5 pounds or less, choose "cut in" boxes, which need not be secured to studs or joists. If wall or ceiling coverings haven't been installed, you can nail a "flange" box to studs or joists. Unless codes prohibit the use of plastic, you may select either plastic or metal boxes. Metal boxes, though sturdier, must be grounded; plastic boxes cost less and need not be grounded.

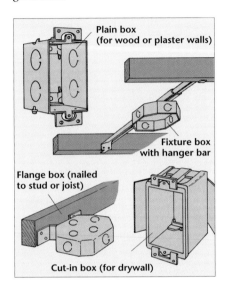

Plain box (for wood or plaster walls)

Fixture box with hanger bar

Flange box (nailed to stud or joist)

Cut-in box (for drywall)

Position the box between studs or joists in an area free of pipes and other wires. To find a suitable location, first cut off power to all circuits that might run behind the wall or ceiling where you're placing the box. Drill a small test hole, and probe behind the surface with a length of stiff wire until you find a large enough space.

Trace the outline of the box on the wall or ceiling, omitting any

protruding brackets. Drill a starter hole in one corner, then make the cutout with a keyhole or saber saw.

Routing new cable.
Your new "wires" actually will be self-contained lengthened nonmetallic sheathed cable. A single cable contains either one or two hot wires, a neutral wire, and a grounding wire, each wrapped in its own insulation. To ensure the best splices, use only cable containing all-copper wire. Check your local electrical codes for the correct cable size.

After cutting the holes but before mounting the boxes, you must run cable from the power source to each new box location. Access from an unfinished basement, an unfloored attic, or a garage adjacent to the kitchen makes it easy to run cable either on top of joists and studs or through holes drilled in them.

If walls and ceilings are covered on both sides, you'll have to "fish" the cable (see drawing below). Use a fish tape (buy it at a plumbing supply or hardware store—or you may find one to rent) or a length of stiff wire. Two "fish" tapes may be needed to pull the wire around corners.

HOW TO ROUTE CABLE TO FIXTURES

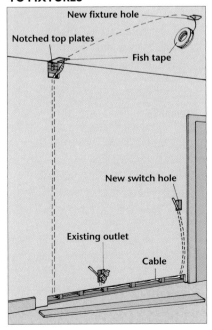

New fixture hole

Notched top plates

Fish tape

New switch hole

Existing outlet

Cable

HOW TO ROUTE CABLE TO OUTLETS

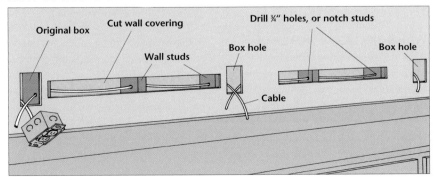

Original box

Cut wall covering

Drill ¾" holes, or notch studs

Wall studs

Box hole

Box hole

Cable

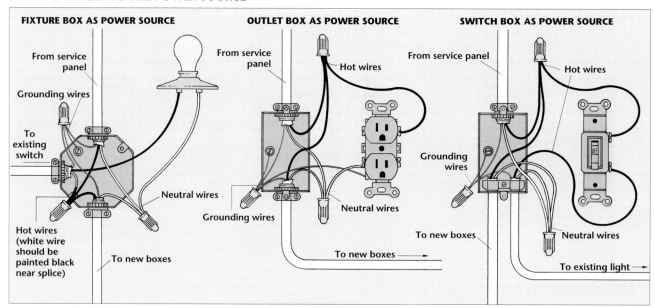

FIXTURE BOX AS POWER SOURCE

From service panel

Grounding wires

To existing switch

Hot wires (white wire should be painted black near splice)

Neutral wires

To new boxes

OUTLET BOX AS POWER SOURCE

From service panel

Hot wires

Grounding wires

Neutral wires

Grounding wires

To new boxes

SWITCH BOX AS POWER SOURCE

From service panel

Hot wires

Grounding wires

Neutral wires

To new boxes

To existing light

Attaching new boxes. After you've routed the new cable, secure each housing box to the ceiling or wall. Slip a cable connector onto the end of the cable and insert it through a knockout in the box. Fasten the connector to the box, leaving 6 to 8 inches of cable free for making the connections. Then mount the box.

Wiring into the power source. Connections to three types of boxes used as power sources are illustrated above. A fourth option is a junction box, where wires are simply joined.

Wirenuts join and protect the stripped ends of spliced wires within housing boxes. The correct wirenut size depends on the number and size of wires you'll be joining.

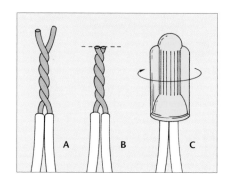

To join wires with a wirenut, follow this sequence: strip 1 inch of insulation from the wire ends and twist the ends clockwise at least 1½ turns (A); snip ⅜ to ½ inch off the twisted wires (B); then screw the wirenut clockwise onto the wires (C).

WIRING PLUG-IN OUTLETS

Plug-in outlets can be wired in several ways. You may want to keep one or both halves electrically live at all times so that appliances can be controlled by their own switches. Or you may wish to turn one or both halves on and off with wall switches—for example, to control a garbage disposer.

Plug-in outlets should be evenly distributed between small appliance circuits in the kitchen area. For example, if there are two small appliance circuits and eight outlets in the area, each circuit should serve four outlets.

All outlets for 15- or 20-amp circuits must be of the grounding type shown at the top of page 81. Outlets are rated for a specific amperage and voltage; be sure to buy the type you need.

If you want to add a grounded outlet to a circuit that does not contain a grounding wire, you may be able to run a separate wire from the new outlet. Check with an electrician.

Most outlets have three different-colored screw terminals. The brass ones are hot, the white or silver ones are neutral, and the green one is the grounding terminal.

The drawings at the top of page 81 show two common ways to wire new outlets. The first, the usual arrangement, has both halves always hot. In the second, the two halves operate independently of each other, with one half controlled by a wall switch (use pliers to remove the break-off ear that connects the outlet's two hot terminals).

The housing boxes are assumed to be metal; if you choose plastic, there's no need to ground the boxes, but you'll have to attach a grounding wire to each outlet. Simply loop the end of the wire under the grounding screw.

An exception to the color code rule

We often assume that a white wire is always a neutral wire. Wires that are black or red are always hot. In some cases, a white wire may substitute as a hot (black) wire. For example, a switch loop can be wired with a two-wire cable that is purchased with one black wire and one white wire, in which case the white wire substitutes as the current-carrying wire going from the source to the switch. A good safety practice is to paint the ends of the hot white wire black.

HOW TO WIRE PLUG-IN OUTLETS

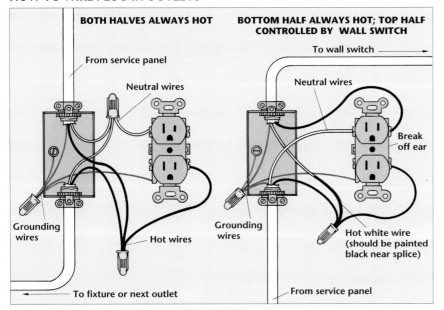

BOTH HALVES ALWAYS HOT

From service panel

Neutral wires

Grounding wires

Hot wires

To fixture or next outlet

BOTTOM HALF ALWAYS HOT; TOP HALF CONTROLLED BY WALL SWITCH

To wall switch

Neutral wires

Break off ear

Grounding wires

Hot white wire (should be painted black near splice)

From service panel

After you have made the wire attachments, fold the wires back into the box and screw the outlet to the box. Adjust the screws in the mounting slots until the outlet is straight. If necessary, shim it out, using either the break-off portions of the outlet's mounting brackets or washers. Finally, add the cover plate.

WIRING 240-VOLT OUTLETS

Because a straight 240-volt circuit has two hot wires, a grounding wire, and no separate neutral wire, you'll need a two-pole, three-wire outlet of the correct amperage. Most models feature push-in terminals, as shown below, left. Using the outlet's strip gauge as a guide, strip insulation from the wire ends, push the wires into the correct terminals, and tighten the screws.

Circuits rated for 120/240 volts have two hot wires and a neutral wire but, depending on whether the circuits originate at the service entrance panel or at a subpanel, they may or may not have a grounding wire.

If the circuit originates at the service entrance panel, check to see if the codes in your area permit you to ground the device connected to it through the neutral wire, which lets you use a three-pole, three-wire outlet. However, if your circuit runs from a subpanel, you must include a separate grounding wire and use a three-pole, four-wire outlet. The drawing below, left shows both situations.

BUILT-IN PROTECTION: THE GFCI

The ground-fault circuit interrupter (GFCI) is a device designed to protect you from electric shocks. The protection value of a GFCI has made it standard equipment in new construction; the NEC requires that all kitchen countertop outlets be equipped with one. Depending on the model, the GFCI may also protect all other outlets downstream (away from the source) from it, but it will not protect any outlets upstream (toward the source).

A GFCI receptacle is wired like an ordinary plug-in outlet. If yours comes with short wires instead of terminals, use wirenuts to splice their free ends to the wires in the box. A typical hookup is shown below.

A LOOK AT 240-VOLT OUTLETS

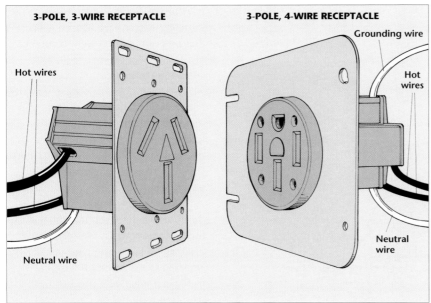

3-POLE, 3-WIRE RECEPTACLE

Hot wires

Neutral wire

3-POLE, 4-WIRE RECEPTACLE

Grounding wire

Hot wires

Neutral wire

HOW TO WIRE A GFCI

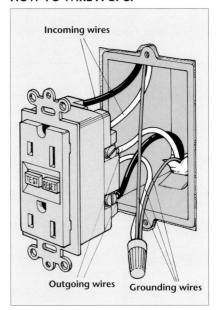

Incoming wires

Outgoing wires

Grounding wires

HOW TO WIRE SINGLE-POLE SWITCHES

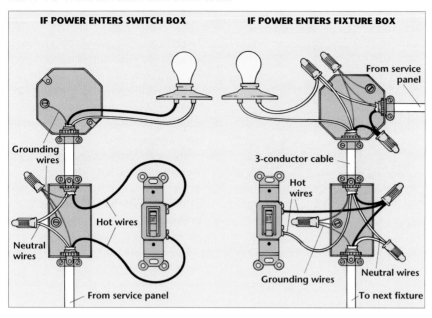

IF POWER ENTERS SWITCH BOX

Grounding wires

Hot wires

Neutral wires

From service panel

IF POWER ENTERS FIXTURE BOX

From service panel

3-conductor cable

Hot wires

Grounding wires

Neutral wires

To next fixture

Single-pole switches. These switches have two screw terminals of the same color (usually brass) for wire connections, and a definite vertical orientation. You should be able to read the words ON and OFF embossed on the toggle. It makes no difference which hot wire goes to which terminal. Because of wiring logistics, the cable sometimes will run to the fixture first and at other times to the switch. Both situations are shown at left.

Three-way switches. These switches have two screw terminals of the same color (brass or silver) and one of a darker color, identified by the word "common." Either end of a three-way switch can go up. It's important to observe, though, which terminal is the odd-colored one; it may be located differently than in the drawing below.

To wire a pair of three-way switches, first connect the hot wire from the service entrance panel or subpanel to the odd-colored terminal of one switch; then connect the hot wire from the fixture or outlet to the odd-colored terminal of the other switch. Wire the remaining terminals by running hot wires from the two same-colored terminals on one switch to the two same-colored terminals on the other.

WIRING NEW SWITCHES

Both "single pole" and "three way" switches are used in homes. A single-pole switch may control one or more light fixtures or outlets; two three-way switches may also control one or more devices.

Like outlets, each switch must have the same amp and voltage rating as the circuit. Remember when wiring

that switches are installed only along hot wires.

Because the plastic toggles used on most home switches are shockproof, these switches do not need to be grounded. However, grounding wires provide an extra safety precaution. If the switches are housed inside metal boxes, the boxes definitely need to be grounded.

INSTALLING DIMMER SWITCHES

Most dimmer switches can be wired into existing circuits in the same way as the switches they replace. The exception is a dimmer for a fluorescent fixture: if available, this type may require extra steps and hardware.

A single-pole switch must be replaced with a single-pole dimmer. If the dimmer comes with short wires instead of terminals, use wirenuts to splice their free ends to the wires in the switch box (for details on using wirenuts, see page 80).

Likewise, if you wish to add a dimmer to a three-way system, replace the three-way switch most frequently used with a three-way dimmer. The wire attached to the common terminal on the switch must be reattached to the common terminal on the dimmer.

TWO WAYS TO WIRE THREE-WAY SWITCHES

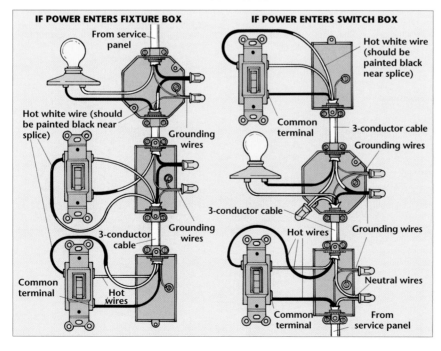

IF POWER ENTERS FIXTURE BOX

From service panel

Hot white wire (should be painted black near splice)

Grounding wires

3-conductor cable

Grounding wires

Common terminal

Hot wires

IF POWER ENTERS SWITCH BOX

Hot white wire (should be painted black near splice)

Common terminal

3-conductor cable

Grounding wires

3-conductor cable

Hot wires

Grounding wires

Neutral wires

Common terminal

From service panel

Light fixtures

Kitchen lighting needs fall into two categories—general and task lighting. Both incandescent and fluorescent lights can be used to satisfy either need. You'll probably implement lighting with one or more of the three popular types of fixtures: surface-mounted, track, and recessed down-light or panel.

Replacing an existing light fixture with one of the same type usually is a minor operation; you simply unscrew the fixture from its housing, disconnect the wires of the old fixture, and hook up new wires. Adding a new fixture where there was none is a more complex process. After running new cable from a power source, you must install a housing box and a switch to control the fixture. Do you feel that's out of your league? For help, see "Electrical basics" on pages 77–82, or consult an electrician.

INSTALLING SURFACE-MOUNTED FIXTURES

Surface-mounted fixtures are either attached directly to a fixture box in the wall or ceiling or suspended from the box by chains or cord. New fixtures usually come with their own mounting hardware, adaptable to any existing fixture box. Sometimes, though, the weight of the new fixture or the wiring necessary for proper grounding requires that you replace the box before installing the fixture.

Attaching fixtures. Most light fixtures can be mounted to a standard ceiling box, which is nailed to a joist or hung on a bracket between joists. Most ceiling fans can also be attached to a standard ceiling box, as long as it is listed for that purpose. Light fixtures and ceiling fans weighing more than 70 pounds require special support.

Grounding metal fixtures. The National Electrical Code requires that all incandescent and fluorescent fixtures with exposed metal parts be grounded.

If the fixture box is not grounded (as in the case when your present house wiring includes no grounding wire), you may be able to extend a grounding wire from the box, but check with an electrician first about the best way to handle the job. Also check your local electrical codes to see if there are any recommendations or any restrictions.

Replacing fixtures. Whether you're replacing an old fixture with the same type or with a new fluorescent unit, the steps are the same.

To begin, disconnect the circuit by removing the fuse or switching the circuit breaker to OFF. Carefully remove any shade from the old fixture. Unscrew the canopy from the fixture box; detach the mounting bar if there is one. Have a helper hold the fixture to keep it from falling and breaking.

Now, make a sketch of how the wires are connected. If they're spliced with wirenuts, unscrew them and untwist the wires. If the wires are spliced only with electrician's tape, simply unwind the tape. New splices will be covered with wirenuts. Lay the old fixtures aside.

As your helper holds up the new fixture, match its wires to the old wires as shown in your sketch. Splice with wirenuts (see page 80).

Secure the new fixture by reversing the steps you took to loosen the original, using any new hardware included with the fixture.

SURFACE-MOUNTED FIXTURES

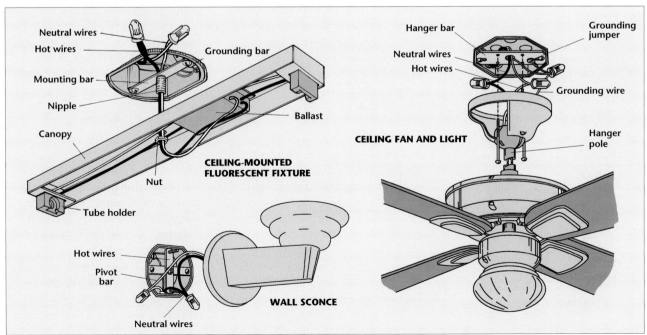

Neutral wires
Hot wires
Mounting bar
Nipple
Canopy
Grounding bar
Ballast
Nut
Tube holder
CEILING-MOUNTED FLUORESCENT FIXTURE

Hot wires
Pivot bar
Neutral wires
WALL SCONCE

Hanger bar
Neutral wires
Hot wires
Grounding jumper
Grounding wire
Hanger pole
CEILING FAN AND LIGHT

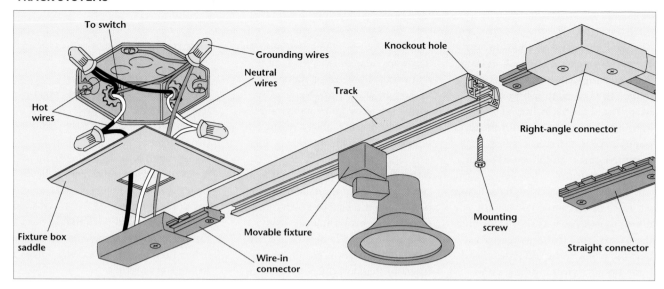

Adding new fixtures. Installing a new surface-mounted fixture is much like replacing one, once the cable has been routed from a power source and the fixture box and switch installed.

New nonmetallic cable routed to the box should include a grounding wire, which is attached to the box's grounding screw. If more than one cable enters the box (for example, a separate cable may be connected to the switch box), you'll need to attach the end of a short length of #12 wire (a "jumper") to the grounding screw

ONE CABLE

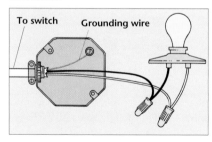

TWO CABLES

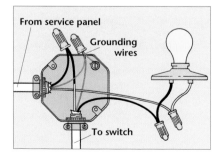

and splice its other end to the ends of the grounding wires in the cables. Cap the splice with a wirenut.

A cord or chain-hung fixture must also have a grounding wire run from the socket to the box. New fixtures are usually prewired with a grounding wire and are ready to hang.

Match the box's wires to those of the new fixture—black wires to black, white to white, as shown on page 83. Cap all splices with wirenuts. Then mount the fixture with the hardware specified by the manufacturer.

INSTALLING TRACK SYSTEMS

Track systems are mounted, either directly or with mounting clips, to the wall or ceiling. Power is provided from a fixture box or through a cord plugged into an existing outlet. Tracks are often wired into two separate circuits controlled by two switches or dimmers.

Low-voltage track fixtures with integral transformers or adapters can be plugged into a standard 120-volt track. Other systems require an external transformer to step down power to the track itself. In this case, you'll need to mount the transformer and then route wire to the track location.

Connecting the system. A plug-in connector, which includes a 12-foot cord and a lamp plug, lets you place a

track wherever the cord will reach an outlet. Plug-in connectors are available only with single-circuit tracks.

A track system with a wire-in connector is hooked up directly to a fixture box. You may be able to use an existing box, or you may have to install a new one (see pages 78–79). In either case, you'll need as many wall switches as your track has circuits. By using a special connector available with some track systems, you can bring in power along a track run rather than at the end.

To install a wire-in connector, position the fixture box saddle and then splice the connector's wires to the incoming cable wires. Cap each splice with a wirenut. Some connectors attach to the fixture box cover; others are simply held in place by the track.

Mounting the track. To attach a track or mounting clips to the ceiling or wall, you'll use screws or toggle bolts in already drilled holes. To lay out and drill the necessary holes, line up a chalkline or the edge of a yardstick with the center slot of the connector; snap or draw a line to the proposed end of the track.

Setting a length of track beside the line, mark along the line the positions of the knockout holes in the roof of the track. These marks show you where to drill.

Because most connectors lie flush against the wall or ceiling surface, you can usually attach the track directly to the surface. Slip the two bare wire ends of the first length of track into the connector receptacles; secure the track with screws or toggle bolts. Proceed in a similar manner with the remaining lengths of track.

Some connectors hold the ends of the track ¼ to ½ inch away from the mounting surface. In this case, you'll need special clips to hold the track at the same level. Once clips are screwed or bolted to the ceiling or wall, slip the first length of track into the connector; press it, and succeeding lengths, into the clips.

INSTALLING RECESSED FIXTURES

Common recessed fixtures include incandescent circular or square downlights and larger fluorescent ceiling, or "troffer," panels. You'll need to cut a hole in the ceiling between the joists, or remove tiles or panels from a suspended ceiling, to install either type. Larger troffer panels may also require 2 by 4 blocking between joists for support.

Recessed fixtures need several inches of clearance above the finished ceiling. They're most easily installed below an unfinished attic or crawlspace. Because of the heat generated by many downlights, you must either buy a special zero-clearance model (type ICT), or plan to remove insulation within 3 inches of the fixture and make sure that no other combustible materials come within ½ inch of the fixture.

Most low-voltage downlights come with an integral transformer attached to the frame; if yours doesn't, you'll first need to mount an external transformer nearby and then route wire to the fixture.

Cutting the ceiling hole. If there's no crawlspace above the ceiling, find the joists (see page 69).

Once you've determined the proper location for the fixture housing, trace its outline on the ceiling with a pencil; use a keyhole saw or saber saw to cut the hole (don't forget to shut off power to any circuits that might be wired behind the ceiling before cutting). Brace a plaster ceiling as you cut.

Mounting the fixture. If you don't have access from above, look for a remodeling fixture. The version shown below, at left, slips through the ceiling hole and clips onto the edge of the ceiling. The fixture trim then snaps onto the housing from below. (Hook up the wires to the circuit before securing the fixture and trim.)

So-called new-work or rough-in downlights with adjustable hanger bars (shown at right) are easy to install from above. Simply nail the ends of the bars to joists on either side; then clip the trim or baffle into place from below.

ADDING UNDERCABINET FIXTURES

One of the most common types of undercabinet lighting, and one of the easiest to install, is an integral fluorescent unit composed of one or two tubes and a ballast. These lights can be permanently wired to a switch or plugged into nearby outlets. For greatest efficiency in providing light, the fixture should span at least two-thirds of the area to be lighted and be mounted as close as possible to the front of the cabinet.

You can also buy lengths of incandescent or halogen strip lights, mounted on metal strips or inside clear plastic tubing. Installation is similar to that of fluorescent units, though you may need to add a low-voltage transformer. These fixtures emit clean, warm lights and are easy to place on a dimmer switch.

Adding a wood or metal valance to a fixture mounted at eye level hides the unit and eliminates glare (see below). Some wall cabinets include this trim; otherwise, measure the required space and cut a piece of cardboard to use as a mockup.

RECESSED DOWNLIGHTS

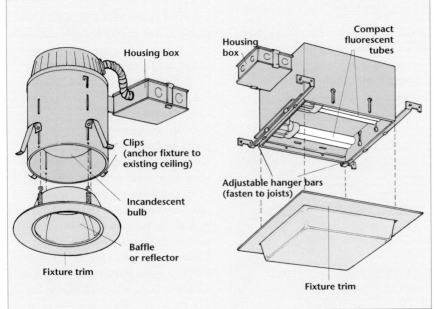

Housing box

Clips (anchor fixture to existing ceiling)

Incandescent bulb

Baffle or reflector

Fixture trim

Housing box

Compact fluorescent tubes

Adjustable hanger bars (fasten to joists)

Fixture trim

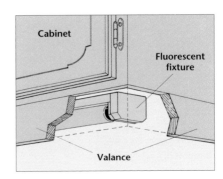

Cabinet

Fluorescent fixture

Valance

Installing new drywall or a suspended ceiling can really change the ambience of your kitchen. Or you can give it a completely new look simply by splashing on a coat of colorful paint or by applying a complementary wall covering.

Fortunately, these improvements are among the easiest projects for the average homeowner to tackle—many of the new products on the market require little or no experience to apply.

INSTALLING DRYWALL

Cutting and installing drywall, also called gypsum wallboard, is a straightforward procedure, but concealing the joints between panels and in the corners demands patience and care. And the weight of full panels can be awkward to negotiate. Drywall is easily damaged; take care not to bend or break the corners or tear the paper covers.

Standard drywall panels are 4 feet wide and from 8 feet to 16 feet long. Common thicknesses are ⅜ inch when used as a backing material for other wall coverings, ½ inch for final wallcoverings, and ⅝ inch where the walls border a garage space. Water-resistant drywall, identified by green or blue paper covers, is designed for areas where heavy moisture might collect.

Cutting drywall. To make a straight cut, first mark the cut line on the front paper layer with a pencil and straightedge, or snap a line with a chalkline. Cut through the front paper with a utility knife as shown below.

Turn the drywall over and break the

INSTALLING DRYWALL ON A WALL

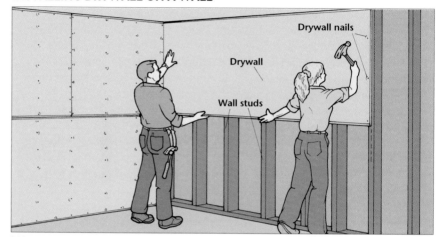

Lift each drywall panel into position and center the edges over wall studs. Then nail or screw the panel to the studs, taking care not to puncture the surface of the drywall. Stagger panels in adjacent rows so that ends don't line up.

gypsum core by bending it toward the back. Finally, cut the back paper along the bend. Smooth the edge of the cut with a perforated rasp.

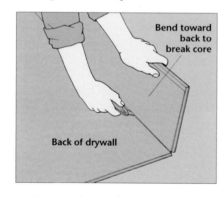

For openings within a panel, drill a pilot hole and make the cutout with a keyhole or drywall saw. Larger edge cutouts should also be made with a keyhole or drywall saw.

When laying out openings or fitting

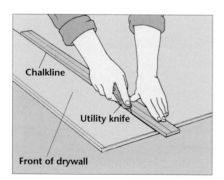

drywall around obstructions such as doorways, carefully measure from the edge of an adjacent drywall panel or reference point to the obstruction. Transfer the measurements to a new panel, then cut out the correct area.

Basic wall application. Wall panels may be positioned either vertically or horizontally—that is, with the long edges either parallel or perpendicular to wall studs. Most professionals prefer the latter method, because it helps bridge irregularities between studs and results in a stronger wall.

But if your wall is higher than 8 feet, you may not want to use this method, since the extra height requires more cutting and creates too many joints.

Before installing drywall panels, mark the stud locations on the floor and ceiling.

Starting at a corner, place the first panel tight against the ceiling and secure it with nails, drywall screws, or construction adhesive supplemented by nails. Drive in nails with a hammer, dimpling the drywall surface without puncturing the paper. Screws are quick and strong, but you'll need a power screw gun or a drill with an adjustable clutch to drive them. Fastener spacings are subject to local codes, but typical nail spacing is every 8 inches along panel

INSTALLING DRYWALL ON A CEILING

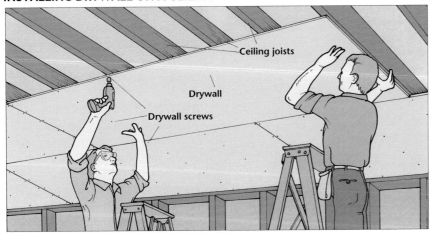

It takes two to install a drywall ceiling. Prop each panel in place with your heads; screw or nail first in the center and that will take the weight off your heads. You can also rent a drywall jack to raise the panels.

ends and edges and along intermediate supports (called "in the field"). Typical screw spacing is every 7 inches along panel ends and at intermediate joists.

Apply additional panels in the same manner. If you're applying drywall horizontally, stagger the end joints in the bottom row so they don't line up with the joints in the top row.

Basic ceiling application. Methods for installing a drywall ceiling are basically the same as those for walls. If you're covering both surfaces, do the ceiling first.

Fasten panels perpendicular to joists with annular ring nails, drywall

screws, or a combination of nails and construction adhesive.

Taping joints and corners. To finish drywall neatly, you'll need drywall tape (buy tape that comes creased) and taping compound.

The taping process is done in stages. To tape a joint between panels, first apply a smooth layer of taping compound over the joint with a 6-inch taping knife. Before the compound dries, embed drywall tape into it and apply a second thin coat of compound over the tape, smoothing it with a knife.

To tape an inside corner, apply a

smooth layer of compound to the drywall on each side of the corner. Measure the length needed and tear the tape, fold it in half vertically along the crease, and press it into the corner with a taping knife or corner tool. Apply a thin layer of compound over the tape and smooth it out.

Exterior corners are covered with a protective metal corner bead and then finished with compound.

Continue taping all the joints. Then, using smooth, even strokes with the 6-inch knife, cover the inside nail dimples with compound.

Allow the taping compound to dry for at least 24 hours before sanding lightly to get a smooth surface. (NOTE: Wear a face mask and goggles while sanding.)

Using a 10-inch knife, apply a second coat of compound, feathering out the edges past each side of the taped joint, making sure it's smooth.

Let the second coat dry. Then sand it and apply a final coat. Use a 10-inch or even wider knife to smooth out and feather the edges, covering all dimples and joints. After the last coat of compound dries, sand it again to remove any minor imperfections.

Textured versus smooth finish. Though many people prefer the smooth look, a texturing coat can hide a less-than-perfect taping job— and add some visual interest to an uninterrupted wall. Some joint compounds can double as texturing compounds, but other effects may require special texturing materials. Ask your dealer to recommend the best materials.

Professionals often apply texturing with a spray gun, but others achieve good results by daubing, swirling, or splattering the compound with a sponge, paint roller, or stiff brush— whatever tool produces the desired appearance.

Let the compound set until slightly stiff; then even it out as required with a wide float or trowel. Allow the finished surface to dry for at least 24 hours before painting.

HOW TO TAPE DRYWALL JOINTS

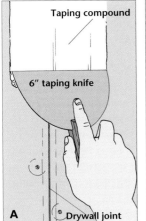
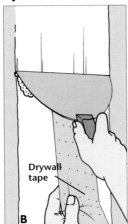
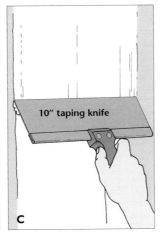

To tape a drywall joint, spread a smooth layer of taping compound over the joint (A), embed paper tape in compound (B), and apply a second, thinner layer of compound. When it's dry, sand smooth and apply a wider layer of compound (C), feathering the edges.

MOLDING JOINTS

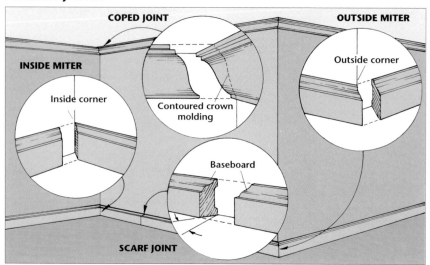

MOLDINGS AND TRIM

The absence of moldings, it's often said, is a sign of good craftsmanship. Even in the most basic room paneled with drywall, though, moldings have their place along the base of walls and around door and window frames; in fact, many traditional architectural styles make extensive decorative use of moldings.

Measuring and cutting. A miter box and backsaw are the traditional tools for neatly cutting trim. But if you're making lots of cuts or working with unusual angles, you may want to borrow or rent a power miter saw. This precision miter saw allows you to cut the trim a bit longer than needed and then nibble fine bits of wood until the joint is perfect.

When you are measuring for miters—for example, to frame a window—measure the precise inside dimensions and cut your material accordingly (that is, adding on the mitered part). Remember that you must reverse the cuts on the ends of each piece of molding.

Contoured moldings may require a coped joint at inside corners for a smooth fit. To form a coped joint, cut the first piece of molding square and butt it into the corner. Then cut the end of the second piece back at a 45° angle, as shown at right. Next, using a coping saw, follow the exposed

curvature of the molding's front edge while reinstating the 90° angle.

Fastening moldings. Unless your molding calls for special adhesive or color-matched fasteners, nail it in place with finishing nails and recess the heads with a nailset. Choose a nail that's at

COPING A JOINT

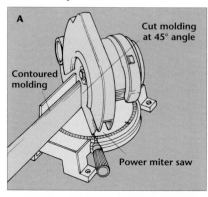

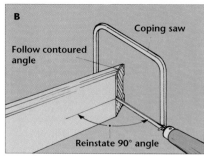

For a coped joint, first miter end at 45° angle, using a power miter saw (A) or a backsaw and miter box. Then follow shape of exposed edge with a coping saw while reinstating original 90° angle (B).

least twice as long as your molding's thickness.

If you'll be painting the trim, fill the holes with wood putty; if you're staining or varnishing, apply a color-matched filler after finishing.

PAINTING YOUR KITCHEN

A fresh coat of paint provides the fastest way to "remodel" your kitchen. Here are some guidelines.

Choosing the paint. Your basic choices are latex and alkyd paint. Latex is easy to work with, and best of all, you can clean up wet paint with soap and water. Alkyd paint (often called oil-based paint) provides high gloss and will hang on a little harder than latex; however, alkyds are trickier to apply than latex and require diligent cleanup with mineral spirits.

Tools of the trade. Choosing the correct brushes is almost as important as selecting the paint. Natural bristles (hog hairs) are traditionally used to apply oil-based paints. They should not be used with latex paint; the bristles soak up water from the paint and quickly become soggy and useless. Synthetic bristles, nylon or nylonlike, are best for applying latex, but most can also be used with oil-base paints.

For window sashes, shutters, and trim, choose a 1½- or 2-inch angled sash brush. For woodwork and other medium-sized surfaces, a 2- or 3-inch brush is best if brushing is your choice for applying the paint.

When you want to paint a large flat area quickly and easily, though, a roller is the answer. A 9-inch roller will handle all interior paint jobs. A handle threaded to accommodate an extension pole will allow you to reach high walls and ceilings without a ladder. The roller's cover is important—choose a nylon blend for latex, lambskin for oil-based paint, or mohair for use with both. A well-designed roller tray is also an essential tool.

Preparing the surface. A key factor in preventing cracking and peeling after the paint dries is preparing the

TOOLS OF THE PAINTING TRADE

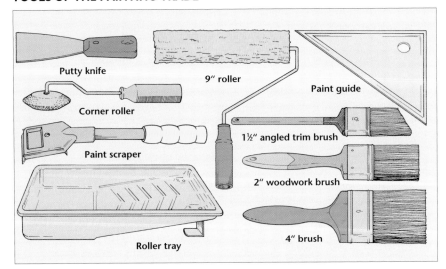

Putty knife

9" roller

Paint guide

Corner roller

Paint scraper

1½" angled trim brush

2" woodwork brush

Roller tray

4" brush

surface correctly. It's essential to the bonding and durability of any latex paint application.

Start by removing light fixtures and faceplates. Then inspect the area you're painting for small holes as well as more extensive damage, and make all necessary repairs.

If an old paint finish is flaking, you must sand it smooth. And when you paint over a glossy surface, you must first roughen the old finish with sandpaper so the new paint will adhere. Use a sponge soaked with paint thinner on any spots that are very greasy. Then an overall dusting, a sponging with an abrasive cleanser, and rinsing (complete a small area at a time) will finish off the surface preparation. Allow about 24 hours for all washed areas to dry completely.

Sometimes an old finish is in such poor condition that the paint must be removed entirely. The easiest method of stripping old paint is to apply a commercial liquid paint remover, then scrape off the softened paint with a broad knife or paint scraper. Finish the surface by sanding lightly until it's clean and smooth.

It's possible to paint over wallpaper that's smooth and attached firmly to the wall. Apply a sealing primer such as pigmented shellac or a flat oil-based enamel undercoat. Let the sealer dry completely before you paint.

It's often safer, though, to remove

the wallpaper, especially if it's tearing and flaking. See "Hanging new wallpaper" at right for details.

Unpainted plaster or drywall should be primed with latex paint or latex primer-sealer. Prime unpainted wood with oil-based paint whether you plan to finish with oil-based or latex.

Painting tips. If you're painting both walls and ceiling, start with the ceiling. Paint the entire ceiling without stopping. You'll want to paint in rectangles, approximately 2 feet by 3 feet, starting in a corner and working across the ceiling in the direction of the shortest distance.

Begin the first section by using a brush, pad applicator, or special corner roller to paint a narrow strip next to the wall line and around any fixtures. Then finish the section with a roller, being careful to overlap any brush marks. Continue painting, one section at a time, from one end of the ceiling to the other and back again.

Then it's on to the walls. Mentally divide a wall into 3-foot-square sections, starting from a corner at the ceiling line and working down the wall. As with ceilings, use a brush, pad applicator, or corner roller along the ceiling line, corners, fixtures, or edges of openings. Finish each section with a roller, being careful to overlap any brush marks.

At the bottom edge along the floor

or baseboard, or along the edges of cabinets and counters, use a brush and paint guide; as before, overlap the brush strokes with a roller. Return to the ceiling line and once again work down the wall in 3-foot sections.

HANGING NEW WALLPAPER

Next to paint, wallpaper is the most popular covering for kitchen walls. Easier than ever to install, wallpaper is available in a kaleidoscope of colors and patterns.

Choices for the kitchen. A wallpaper for the kitchen should be durable, stain resistant, and able to be scrubbed. Solid vinyl wallpapers, available in a wide variety of colors and textures, fill the bill. Vinyl coatings also give wallpaper a washable surface but aren't notably durable or grease resistant.

If you're a beginner, you may want to consider using a prepasted and pretrimmed paper.

To find an adhesive suitable for your material, check the manufacturer's instructions or ask your dealer.

Preparing the surface. To prepare for papering, you'll need to remove all light fixtures and faceplates. Thoroughly clean and rinse the surface. Most manufacturers recommend that you completely remove any old wallpaper before hanging a nonporous covering like solid vinyl.

If the existing paper is strippable, it will come off easily when you pull it up at a corner or seam. To remove nonstrippable wallpaper, use either a steamer (available for rent from your dealer) or a spray bottle filled with very hot water. (Steaming can damage plaster walls, so test it first on a small area.) Before steaming, break the surface of the old paper by sanding it with very coarse sandpaper or by pulling a sawblade sideways across the wall.

Within a few minutes of steaming (wait longer if it's a nonporous material), you can begin to remove the old paper. Using a broad knife, work down from the top of the wall, scraping off the old wallpaper as thoroughly as possible.

If yours is a new drywall surface, tape all joints between panels (see page 87) before papering. When dry, sand the wall smooth and apply a coat of flat, oil-based primer-sealer.

If you want to apply wallpaper over previously painted surfaces that are in good condition, simply clean off all the dirt, grease, and oil, and let it dry. If latex paint was used, or if you can't determine the type, you must apply an oil-based undercoat over the old paint.

Ready to start? Plan the best place to hang your first strip. If you are papering all four walls with patterned paper, the last strip you hang probably won't match the first, so plan to start and finish in the least conspicuous place—usually a corner, entry door casing, or window casing.

Most house walls are not straight and plumb, so you'll need to establish a plumb line. Figure the width of your first strip of wallpaper minus ½ inch (which will overlap the corner or casing); measure that distance from your starting point, and mark the wall. Using a carpenter's level as a straightedge, draw a line through your mark that's perfectly plumb. Extend the line until it reaches from floor to ceiling.

It's a good idea to measure the wall height before cutting each strip of wallpaper. Allow 2 inches extra at the top and bottom. Be sure also to allow for pattern match.

Using a razor knife, cut the strips. Number them on the back at the top edge so you can apply them in the proper sequence.

With some wallpapers, you'll need to spread adhesive on the backing with a wide, soft paint roller or pasting brush; other papers are prepasted—all you have to do is soak them in water before hanging.

After pasting or soaking, strips should be "booked," as shown below, until ready to hang.

BOOKING WALLPAPER

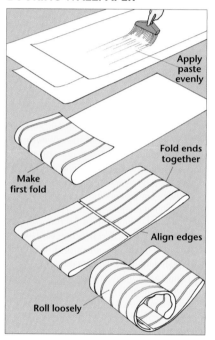

Apply paste evenly

Make first fold

Fold ends together

Align edges

Roll loosely

Trim the edges of the wallpaper at this stage, if necessary. You're now ready to hang the paper.

Hanging the wallpaper. First, position a stepladder next to the plumb line you've marked. Open the top fold of the first booked strip, raising it so that it overlaps the ceiling line by 2 inches. Carefully align the strip's edge with the plumb line.

Using a smoothing brush, press the strip against the wall. Smooth out all wrinkles and air bubbles. Then release the lower portion of the strip and smooth it into place.

Carefully roll the edges flat, if necessary, with a seam roller. To trim along the ceiling and baseboard, use a broad knife and a very sharp razor knife. With a sponge dipped in lukewarm water, remove any excess adhesive before it dries.

Unfold your second strip on the wall in the same way you did the first. Gently butt the second strip against the first, aligning the pattern as you move down the wall. In this manner, continue around the room applying the remaining strips of paper.

Dealing with corners. Because few rooms have perfectly straight corners, you'll have to measure from the edge of the preceding strip to the corner; do this at three heights.

HANGING THE FIRST STRIP

 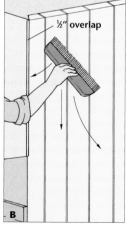  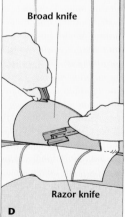 

2" overlap

Plumb line

A

½" overlap

B

Seam roller

C

Broad knife

Razor knife

D

Sponge

E

To hang wallpaper, first open the top fold of the strip, overlap the ceiling line, and align the strip's edge with the plumb line (A); press the strip against the wall with a smoothing brush (B). Release the lower fold and smooth into place; roll the edges flat with a seam roller (C). Trim the strip along the ceiling and baseboard with a broad knife and a razor knife (D). Remove excess adhesive with a sponge dipped in lukewarm water (E).

Cut a strip ½ inch wider than the widest measurement. Butting the strip to the preceding strip, brush it firmly into and around the corner. At the top and bottom corners, cut the overlap so the strip will lie flat.

Next, measure the width of the leftover piece of wallpaper. On the adjacent wall, measure the same distance from the corner and make a plumb line at that point.

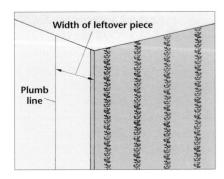

Position one edge of the strip along the plumb line; the other edge will cover the ½-inch overlap. (If you're hanging vinyl wallpaper, you should apply a vinyl-to-vinyl adhesive on top of the overlap.)

Cutouts. It's easy to cut around electrical switches and plug-in outlets. Be sure all faceplates have been removed before hanging the wallpaper; then, before making the cutout for the faceplate, shut off the electricity.

Hang the paper as described above. Then use a razor knife to make an X-shaped cut over the opening, extending the cuts to each corner. Trim the excess along the edges of the opening with the razor knife and a broad knife.

INSTALLING A SUSPENDED CEILING

Easy-to-install suspended ceilings consist of a metal grid suspended from above with wire or spring-type hangers. The grid holds acoustic or decorative or fiberboard panels.

The most common panel size is 2 feet by 4 feet, though panels are available in a variety of sizes. Transparent and translucent panels and egg-crate grilles are made to fit the gridwork to

INSTALLING A SUSPENDED CEILING

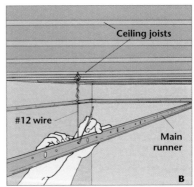

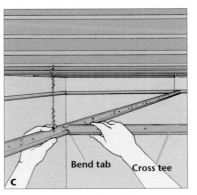

To hang a suspended ceiling, snap a chalkline around the room and install L-shaped molding with its base on the chalkline (A). Set the main runners on the molding at each end, attach them to the joists with #12 wire (B), lock 4-foot cross tees to the main runners (C). Push the panels through the grid and drop them into place (D).

admit light from above. Recessed lighting panels that exactly replace one panel also are available from some manufacturers. All components are replaceable, and the panels can be raised for access to the area above.

Figuring your needs. Here is the easiest way to determine the number of panels you'll need. Measure your wall lengths at the proposed ceiling height. Draw the ceiling area to scale on graph paper, using one square per foot of ceiling size. Block in the panel size you'll be using. Finally, count the blocked areas and parts of areas to get the number of panels you'll need.

For a professional-looking job, plan equal borders on the opposite sides of the room. To determine the nonstandard width of panels needed for perimeter rows, measure the extra space from the last full row of panels to one wall and divide by two. This final figure will be the dimension of border tiles against that wall and the

opposite wall. Repeat this procedure for the other room dimensions.

Installing the ceiling. First, figure the ceiling height—at least 3 inches below plumbing, 5 inches below lights (minimum ceiling height is 7 feet 6 inches). Snap a chalkline on the walls at that level around the room and install L-shaped angle molding with the base angle molding on the chalkline.

Next, install the main runners perpendicular to the ceiling joists (see above). Cut the runners to length with tin snips. Setting them on the molding at each end, support them every 4 feet with #12 wire attached to small eyebolts screwed into joists above. Lock 4-foot cross tees to the main runners by bending the tabs in the runner spots.

Set the panels into place and install any recessed lighting panels. Cut border panels as necessary with a utility knife and straightedge.

Refacing cabinets

Refacing cabinets gives your kitchen a bright new life for considerably less than the cost of new cabinets. It reuses the old cabinets and you can continue to use your kitchen while the work is being done.

PAINTING CABINETS

One easy way to resurface cabinets is to paint them. You will have to remove the doors and drawers and hardware. Clean the wood, fill any holes with wood putty, and sand all areas. Paint the inside of the cabinets first, then the face frames. Paint the doors and drawers separately. You can reinstall them with new hardware for an entirely new look.

REFACING WITH VENEER

This process entails covering the cabinet frames with adhesive wood veneer and replacing the old cabinet doors and drawers with new ones.

Researching materials. You will need new doors and drawer fronts, matching ¼-inch plywood and self-adhesive veneer, hinges, door knobs, and drawer pulls. There are several places to buy the materials. Many home centers have cabinet doors and drawer fronts, but sizes and choices of wood are limited. If you plan to buy them there, make sure you can get veneer to match and can stain plywood to match. Solid wood and plywood react to stain differently, so you have to test them first. Or, you can order all the materials from a cabinetmaker. It will cost more but you'll have more choices and everything will match. You can

purchase a refacing kit that includes all the necessary materials. Also check refacing contractors to see if they will sell the materials alone without installation.

Measuring the cabinets. It is very important to measure carefully and accurately. Measure the height and width of each door and drawer front. Make a sketch of the cabinets and write the measurements on the sketch. For the veneer, add up the surface area of the cabinet frames and add 15 to 20 percent to the total. Veneer comes in 2 by 8 foot sheets so you can determine how many sheets you will need. Double and triple check all your measurements before ordering any materials.

Preparing the cabinets. Remove the doors and drawer fronts. Repair any cracked or broken cabinet frames. If the face frame extends beyond the end panel, trim off the overhanging "ears" with a router and flushcutting bit, or with a sharp block plane.

Attaching the plywood. Plywood is used to cover all cabinet surfaces too large for veneer: the bottom of upper cabinets, the end wall, and the toe-kick area. The edge of the plywood has to be even with the face frame so the veneer can cover both. When applying contact cement to the back of the plywood to attach it to the cabinet, use a mask and ventilate the room.

Preparing the face frames. To remove dirt from the face frames, lightly sand

them, then wash with mild dishwashing detergent and rinse. Sand joints and newly installed plywood. Fill cracks or holes with wood filler. Spray face frames with a clear aerosol lacquer, using a piece of cardboard to prevent the cabinet insides from being sprayed. Work in a well-ventilated room and wear a mask.

Applying the veneer. Work slowly and carefully with veneer. Once it's in place, it's difficult if not impossible to remove. Begin in an inconspicuous place such as the bottom of a base cabinet to familiarize yourself with the materials.

Measure each face front and cut the veneer ¼ inch wider and ½ inch longer than needed. A long piece can be trimmed; a short piece is wasted. To cut the veneer, use a sharp-bladed utility knife and a metal straightedge, working on a hard surface, not cardboard. Test the fit of each strip, then peel the backing paper off one corner, align it, and press it, peeling off the backing as you go. Use a hard-rubber roller to press the veneer in place. Trim with a snap-blade wallpaper knife. Later you can use a fine-toothed file or fine sandpaper to smooth the edges.

Installing doors and drawers. Install the doors so they are level and with consistent spacing between them. Snap a level chalkline on the face frame above the tops of door openings. Hang doors to this line so cabinets will look uniform even if the openings are slightly out of square. Attach drawer fronts following the manufacturer's instructions.

APPLYING VENEER

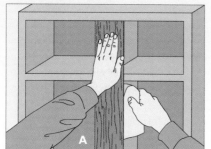 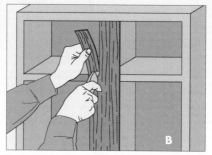 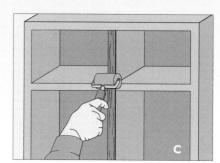

Peel off one corner of the veneer backing, align it on the face frame, and press it in place, removing the backing paper as you go (A). Use a snap-blade wallpaper knife to trim the veneer even with the edges of the face frame (B). Use a hard-rubber roller to press the veneer in place and activate the adhesive (C).

Installing new cabinets and dressing them up with the countertops of your choice can be the passport to a whole new world of kitchen style and efficiency.

Removing and installing cabinets and countertops is not difficult and requires only basic hand tools. But the work must be done carefully to ensure a professional-looking fit.

REMOVING OLD CABINETS

If you remove base cabinets first, you'll have room to get underneath any wall cabinets without strain, and you'll avoid damaging walls or cabinets.

Base cabinets. First, pry away any vinyl wall base, floor covering, or molding from the base cabinet's kickspace or sides as shown above. Next, disconnect plumbing supply lines and the drain trap from the kitchen sink (see page 105). Stuff a rag in the drainpipe to block sewer gas. Also disconnect plumbing and electrical lines to a dishwasher or garbage disposer (see page 106), gas or electric range, wall ovens, or cooktop (see page 109). Be sure plumbing and gas lines and electrical circuits are properly shut off before disconnecting them. Remove sink, fixtures, and appliances.

Old base cabinets are usually attached to wall studs with screws or nails through nailing strips at the back of each unit. Sometimes they're also fastened to the floor with nails through the kickspace trim or cabinet sides. Screws are easy to remove unless they're old and stripped. To remove nails, you may need to pry the cabinet away from the wall or floor with a pry bar. It's best to use a wood scrap between the pry bar and the wall or floor to prevent any damage to those surfaces.

Several base units may be fastened together and covered with a single countertop. If you can remove the entire assembly intact, you'll save time and labor. Otherwise, unscrew or pry the units apart—they're fastened either through adjacent sides or face frames—and remove the countertop.

CABINET ANATOMY

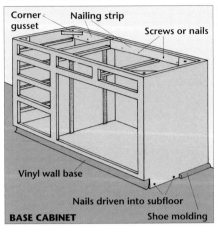

BASE CABINET

Corner gusset — Nailing strip — Screws or nails — Vinyl wall base — Nails driven into subfloor — Shoe molding

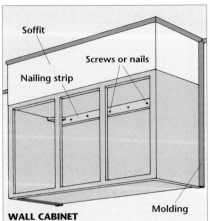

WALL CABINET

Soffit — Screws or nails — Nailing strip — Molding

Countertops typically are anchored to the cabinet frame from below, through rails or corner gussets. Plastic laminate, hardwood butcher block, and the backing for ceramic tile countertops are normally fastened with screws; masonry and synthetic marble are attached with adhesive.

Wall cabinets. Once the base cabinets are out of the way, you're ready to remove the wall cabinets. They're either screwed, bolted, or nailed through nailing strips at the backs of the cabinets to wall studs behind each unit. They might also be fastened to the ceiling or an overhead soffit.

If the cabinets are screwed or bolted to the wall, recruit some helpers to hold them in place while you unfasten them. Then remove the cabinets from the area. If the cabinets are fastened with nails, you'll have to use a pry bar. Again, individual units are probably fastened together. If you have a helper or two, the cabinet assembly can often be removed intact.

INSTALLING NEW CABINETS

Both wall and base cabinets are carefully aligned with layout marks previously drawn on the walls. Then they're fastened to studs with screws. In order to give yourself adequate working room and prevent damage to base cabinets, it's usually simpler to install wall cabinets first.

Wall cabinets. Your first task is to locate and mark wall studs in the area of your new cabinets. (For help in finding studs, see page 69.)

Next you'll need to lay out lines on the wall for the top and bottom of the cabinets. Measure up 84 inches from the floor (the standard top height for wall cabinets). Because floors are seldom completely level, measure in several spots and use the highest mark as your reference point. Trace a line from this mark across the wall, using a carpenter's level as a straightedge.

Now subtract the exact height of the new cabinet units from the top line and mark this line on the wall. Screw a temporary ledger strip made from 1 by 4 lumber to the wall studs, with the ledger's top edge exactly flush with the bottom line.

Start your cabinet installation either from a corner of the kitchen or from any full-height cabinet. You can determine the location of the latter from your kitchen plans. Again, mark the wall.

Remove cabinet doors by their hinge pins, if possible. Then, with as much help as you can recruit, lift the first cabinet into place atop the ledger strip. While your helpers hold the cabinet into position, drill pilot holes through the top and bottom nailing strips and into wall studs; loosely fasten the cabinet to the studs with wood screws long enough to extend 1½ inches into the studs when tight.

CABINET REFERENCE LINES

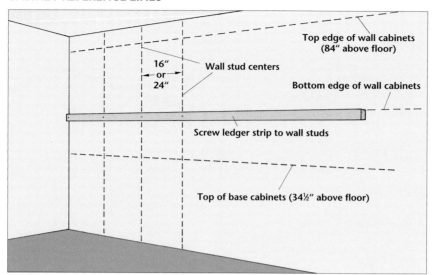

Top edge of wall cabinets (84" above floor)

16" or 24"

Wall stud centers

Bottom edge of wall cabinets

Screw ledger strip to wall studs

Top of base cabinets (34½" above floor)

At this point, careful attention to detail will ensure a first-rate installation. Check the cabinet carefully to make sure it is level and plumb—from top to bottom and from front to back—with your carpenter's level. Because walls seldom are exactly plumb, you may have to make some fine adjustments to enable the cabinet to hang correctly. Bumps and high points on the wall can sometimes be sanded down; low points will need to be shimmed.

Drive shims as needed between the cabinet back and the wall, either down from the top or in from the side. Tap the shims in a little at a time, and keep checking with the level. When all is in order, tighten the wood screws; then recheck with the level. If the tightening has thrown the cabinet out of plumb, shim again.

Some cabinets are designed with "scribing strips" along the sides. Others come with decorative panels that finish the visible end of a cabinet run. Both cabinet designs include extra material you can shave down to achieve a perfect fit between the end cabinet and an irregular wall.

To scribe a cabinet, first position it; then run a length of masking tape down the side to be scribed. Setting the points of a compass with a pencil to the widest gap between the scribing strip and the wall, run the compass pivot down the wall next to the strip, as shown above right. The irregularities in

the wall will be marked on the tape. Remove the cabinet from the wall and use a block plane, file, or power belt sander to trim the scribing strip to the line. Then reinstall the cabinet.

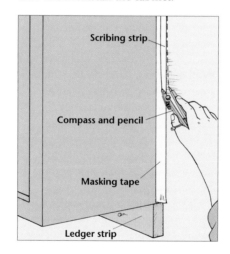

Scribing strip

Compass and pencil

Masking tape

Ledger strip

If your cabinets don't have scribing strips or panels, you can cover any large irregularities with decorative molding or latex caulk.

Adjacent wall cabinets may be joined together on the wall or on the floor; clamp them together with C-clamps, carefully align the front edges, and screw together adjacent cabinet sides or face frames, as shown at right.

Base cabinets. Though base cabinets are less awkward to position than wall cabinets, you must now deal with the vagaries of both wall and floor.

Before you begin, remove any trim,

baseboard, moldings, or wall base that might interfere. From the floor, measure up 34½ inches—the height of a standard base cabinet.

Again, take several measurements and use the highest mark for your reference point. Draw a level line through the mark and across the length of the wall.

If you need to cut access holes in a cabinet's back or bottom for plumbing supply and drain pipes, or for electrical wire serving the sink complex, you'll want to do so before you install the cabinet.

With helpers, move the cabinet into position, threading any plumbing connections or wiring through the access holes. Measure the cabinet carefully for level and plumb—from side to side and front to back. Then shim the unit as necessary between the cabinet base and floor.

Scribing strips may be included along the sides to allow full alignment with the wall. Both shims and any irregularities in the floor can be hidden by baseboard trim, vinyl wall base, or new flooring.

When the cabinet is aligned, drill pilot holes through the nailing strip at the back of the cabinet into the wall studs. Secure the unit with wood screws or drywall screws.

Once installed, base cabinets are fastened together like wall cabinets; screw together the adjacent sides or face frames. Now it's time to install the new countertop.

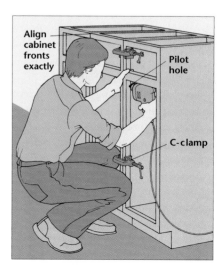

Align cabinet fronts exactly

Pilot hole

C-clamp

INSTALLING PLASTIC LAMINATE COUNTERTOPS

Plastic laminate countertops, the most common countertops used in kitchens, can be divided into two types: post-formed and custom countertops.

Post-formed countertops are molded one-piece tops, from curved backsplash to bullnosed front. They're available in several standard lengths (usually from 6 to 12 feet) and can be cut to the exact length you need. Most types are offered with accessory kits for endsplashes (where the countertop meets a side wall or cabinet) and endcaps.

With a custom plastic laminate countertop, you apply the laminate of your choice over an old countertop or new core material. Though post-formed countertops are simpler to install, building your own enables you to choose from a much greater selection of laminates. You can also tailor the dimensions of the backsplash, endsplash, and overhang to your exact requirements.

Post-formed countertops. Since post-formed countertops come only in standard sizes, you'll normally need to buy one slightly larger than you need and cut it to length. To cut the countertop with a handsaw, mark the cut line on the face. Mark the back if you're using a power saw. Use masking tape to protect the cutting line against chipping (you'll probably have to draw the line again, this time on the tape). Smooth the edge of the cut with a file or sandpaper. Plan to cover that end with an endcap or endsplash.

Exactly what size do you need? The standard overhang on a laminate top varies between ¾ inch and 1 inch in front and on open ends. Add these dimensions to the dimensions of your cabinet. If you plan to include an endsplash at one or both ends, check the endsplash kit: since most endsplashes are assembled directly above the end of the cabinet, you generally subtract ¾ inch from the length of the countertop on that side.

POST-FORMED LAMINATE COUNTERTOP

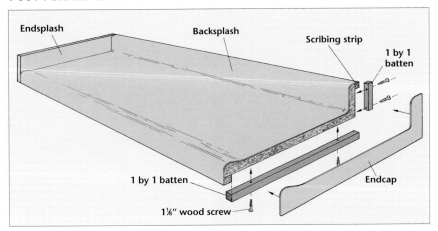

Endsplashes are screwed either directly into the edge of the countertop or into "built down" wood battens previously attached to the edge, as shown above. Apply silicone sealant to the surfaces to be joined. Holding the endsplash in place with C-clamps, drill pilot holes if needed and drive in the screws.

Endcaps (shaped strips of matching laminate) are glued to an open end with contact cement or, in some cases, pressed into place with a hot iron. Again, you first may need to build down the edge with wood battens. File the edges of the new strip flush with the top and front edges of the countertop, or use an electric router and laminate-trimming bit.

If your cabinets are U-shaped or L-shaped, you'll need to buy mitered countertop sections or have them cut to order. (It's very difficult to cut accurate miters at home.) The mitered sections should have small slots along the bottom edges. They are connected with

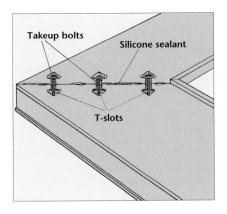

takeup or draw bolts, as shown below.

Coat the mitered edges with silicone sealant, align them carefully, and tighten the bolts. Fasten the backsplashes together with wood screws.

Countertops, like cabinets, rarely fit uniformly against the back or side walls because the walls seldom are straight. Usually the back edge of a post-formed countertop comes with a scribing strip that can be trimmed to follow the exact contours of the wall. Follow the instructions for scribing cabinets detailed on page 94.

Position the countertop on the cabinet frame. Carefully check with a level—across the front and from front to back. Also make sure you can freely open and close the cabinet doors and top drawers with the countertop overhang in place. You may need to add shims or wood blocks around the perimeter and along cross-members of the cabinet top to level or raise the surface for a perfect fit.

Fasten the countertop to the cabinets by running screws from below through the cabinet corner gussets or top frame (see the drawing on page 93) and through any shims or wood blocks. Use wood screws just long enough to penetrate ½ inch into the countertop core. Run a bead of silicone sealant along all exposed seams between the countertop and walls; clean up any excess. If you need to cut a hole in the new countertop for a sink or cooktop, you'll need a keyhole or saber saw and a drill for pilot holes. See page 105 for more details.

CUSTOM LAMINATE COUNTERTOP

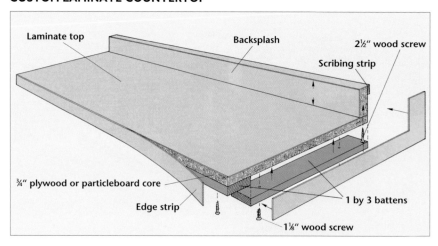

Laminate top • Backsplash • 2½" wood screw • Scribing strip • ¾" plywood or particleboard core • Edge strip • 1 by 3 battens • 1⅛" wood screw

Custom laminate countertops.
To build your own laminate countertop, you'll need to choose the laminate (¹⁄₁₆-inch thickness is the standard) and cut the core material to size from ¾-inch plywood or high-density particleboard.

Build down the edges of the core with 1 by 3 battens (see drawing above). Then you can laminate the countertop. Work on the sides and front strips first and then the top surface.

Measure each surface to be laminated, adding at least ¼ inch to all dimensions as a margin for error. Mark the cutting line. Score the line with a sharp utility knife; then cut with a fine-toothed saw (face up with a handsaw or table saw, face down with a circular saw or saber saw). A laminate cutter is ideal.

Apply contact cement to both the laminate back and core surface to be joined, and allow the cement to dry for 20 to 30 minutes. Carefully check alignment before joining the two; once joined, the laminate can't be moved. Press the laminate into place, using a roller or a rolling pin to ensure even contact between the laminate and core.

Use a block plane to trim the laminate flush with the core's edges; then dress it with a file. Or trim with an electric router equipped with a laminate-trimming bit.

Backsplashes or endsplashes should be cut from the same core material as the main countertop, then butt joined to the countertop using both a sealant and wood screws.

INSTALLING CERAMIC TILE COUNTERTOPS

Wall tiles, which are lighter and thinner than floor tiles, are the normal choice for countertops and backsplashes. Standard sizes range from 3 inches by 3 inches to 4½ inches by 8½ inches, with thicknesses varying from ¼ to ⅜ inch thick. Another choice, mosaic tiles, makes your job easier, especially in backsplash areas.

Preparing the base.
Before laying tile, remove any old countertops (see page 93); then install ¾-inch exterior plywood, cut flush with the cabinet top, screwing it to the cabinet frame from below. For moisture-tight results, add a waterproof membrane and follow it with a layer of cement backerboard on top.

Surfaces may need to be primed or sealed before tile is applied. To determine the best base and preparation for your job, read the information on the adhesive container or ask your tile supplier.

Planning your layout.
Before you start laying tile, decide how you want to trim the countertop edge and sink. For ideas, see drawing below.

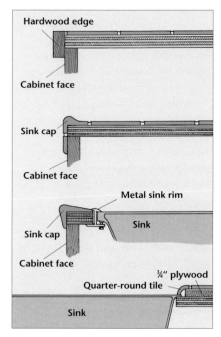

Hardwood edge • Cabinet face • Sink cap • Cabinet face • Metal sink rim • Sink • Sink cap • Cabinet face • ¾" plywood • Quarter-round tile • Sink

If you decide to use wood trim, seal the wood and attach it to the cabinet face with finishing nails. When in place, the wood strip's top edge should be positioned at the

HOW TO SET COUNTERTOP TILES

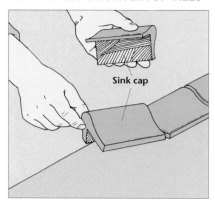

Sink cap

First, set edge tiles in place, starting from the center line, after buttering the backs with adhesive.

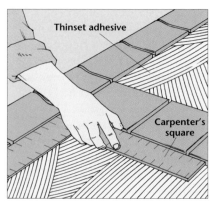

Thinset adhesive • Carpenter's square

Next, install field tiles. Use a square to keep the tiles perpendicular to the edge trim.

same height as the finished tile. A recessed sink is also installed at this time (see page 105).

On the front edge of your plywood base, locate and mark the point where the center of the sink or the midpoint of a blank countertop will be. Lay the edge tiles out on the countertop, starting from your mark. Some tiles have small ceramic lugs molded onto their edges to keep spacing equal; if your tiles don't, use plastic spacers, available from your tile supplier.

Carefully position the rest of the "field" tiles on the countertop. Observing the layout, make any necessary adjustments to eliminate narrow cuts or difficult fits.

If the countertop will have a backsplash or will turn a corner, be sure to figure the cove or corner tiles into your layout.

Mark reference points of your layout on the plywood base to help you recreate it later; then remove all the tiles you placed.

Setting the tiles. Set all trim tiles before spreading adhesive for the field tiles. Thinset adhesive, mixed with latex additive, is water resistant and easy to use.

Butter the back of each front-edge tile and press it into place, aligning it with the reference marks. If your edge trim consists of two tile rows, set the vertical piece first.

Next, butter the backs of cove tiles and set them against the wall. If you've installed a recessed sink, next lay the sink trim. Be sure to caulk between the sink and the base before setting the trim. If you're using quarter-round trim, you can either miter the corners or use special corner pieces available with some patterns.

Next, spread adhesive over a section of the countertop (for information about tools and techniques, see page 100). Begin laying the field tiles, working from front to back. Cut tiles to fit as necessary. As you lay the tiles, check the alignment frequently with a carpenter's square.

To set the tiles and level their faces, slide a 1-foot-square scrap of cloth-covered plywood over them and tap the scrap with a rubber hammer.

Now set the backsplash, beginning one grout joint space above the cove tiles or countertop tiles. Cover the backsplash area with adhesive; for a better grip, you can also butter the back of each tile.

Unless you're tiling up to an overhead cabinet or window sill, use bullnosed tiles for the last row. If a wall contains electrical switches or plug-in outlets, you can cut tiles in two and use tile nippers to nip out a hole.

Applying the grout. Remove any spacers and clean the tile surface and grout joints until they're free of adhesive. Allow thinset adhesive to

set for 24 hours before grouting the joints. For details on grouting tools and techniques, see page 101.

INSTALLING SOLID-SURFACE COUNTERTOPS

Some solid-surface materials can be cut and joined using woodworking techniques—you'll need power tools and carbide-tipped blades to do the job well. Note, however, that many distributors won't sell solid-surface materials unless they do both the fabrication and the installation.

Blanks used for countertops usually range from $\frac{1}{2}$ to $\frac{3}{4}$ inch thick. The $\frac{1}{2}$-inch thickness must be continuously supported by the cabinet frame or closely spaced plywood blocks. If you're installing a sink, you need to add cross-members to the frame for support.

When the slab is cut, it must be firmly supported throughout its length and protected on the cutting line with masking tape.

The countertop can be edged with wood trim, strips of solid-surface material, or a combination of these.

Solid surfacing is very heavy and not an easy material to work with. All of the steps described above should be performed by someone with a great deal of experience using this material. Most often that is a professional installer.

INSTALLING WOOD COUNTERTOPS

Handsome and natural, wood countertops are easy to install. Classic wood butcher-block tops, laminated from strips of hardwood laid on edge, are sold in 24-, 30-, and 36-inch widths and incremental lengths. If required, cut your top to size with a power saw, easing sharp edges and corners with a sander, file, or electric router and roundover bit. Fasten the countertop to cabinets with screws from below. Run a bead of silicone caulk along the seam between the countertop and walls.

You can seal the wood with mineral oil, but you must seal both sides or the counter may warp.

HOW TO SET BACKSPLASH TILES

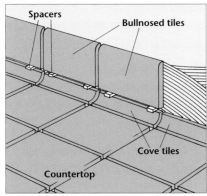

Align joints of backsplash tiles with tiles on the countertop; finish the top with bullnosed tiles.

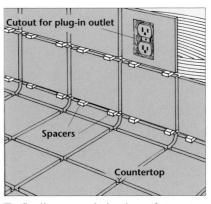

To fit tiles around plug-in outlets, cut a hole in the tile or cut the tile in two and nibble out a hole.

Flooring manufacturers are always improving their wares. They often change the selection and revise the materials, making floors easier to care for and install.

Two primary requirements for a kitchen floor are moisture resistance and durability. Resilient flooring, ceramic tile, laminate flooring, and properly sealed hardwood strips are all good choices.

The information in this section applies to floors that are supported by a standard subfloor, with joists or beams below (for an illustration, see page 67). If you're working in a house that's on a concrete slab, you may have to make special preparations to the slab to ensure that it is perfectly dry before you begin.

RESILIENT SHEET FLOORING

Resilient sheet flooring can be laid in adhesive or placed loosely on the floor like wall-to-wall carpet. Though some types are available in widths up to 12 feet, most sheet flooring is 6 feet wide and may require seaming.

Preparing the subfloor. Both old resilient floors and wood floors make acceptable bases for new resilient sheets, provided their surfaces are completely smooth and level. Old resilient flooring must be the solid, not the cushioned type, and firmly bonded to the subfloor. Uneven wood floors may need a rough sanding (see page 103). Both types of flooring must be thoroughly cleaned before you begin.

Old flooring in poor condition or flooring of ceramic tile or masonry should be removed, if possible, down to the subfloor.

If it is impossible to remove flooring without damaging the subfloor or if the subfloor is in poor condition, cover the old flooring with ¼-inch underlayment-grade plywood, untempered hardboard, or particleboard. Leave a ¹⁄₁₆-inch gap between panels to allow for later expansion. Fasten the panels down with 3-penny ring-shank or 4-penny cement-coated nails spaced 3 inches apart along the edges and 6 inches apart across the face of each panel.

Planning the new floor. Take exact measurements of the kitchen floor and make a scale drawing on graph paper. If your room is very irregular, you may want to make a full-size paper pattern of the floor instead of the scale drawing. To cover a large area, you may need to seam two pieces.

Installing flooring without seams. The most critical step in laying sheet flooring is making the first rough cuts in the material accurately.

Unroll the flooring in a large room or in a clean garage or basement. Transfer the floor plan—or paper pattern—directly onto the top of the flooring, using chalk or a water-soluble felt-tip pen, and with a carpenter's square and a large straightedge for accuracy.

Using a linoleum or utility knife or heavy-duty scissors, cut the flooring roughly 3 inches oversized on all sides. The excess will be trimmed away after the flooring has been positioned.

If adhesive is required with your flooring, it can either be spread over the entire subfloor or, depending on the type of adhesive, spread in steps as the flooring is unrolled. Check the adhesive's "open time"—the time it takes to dry—to choose a method.

Remove the baseboards and molding from walls and cabinet fronts. Carry the roll of flooring into the kitchen and

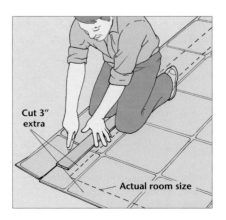

Cut 3" extra

Actual room size

lay the longest edge against the longest wall, allowing the 3-inch excess to curl up the wall. The flooring should also curl up each adjoining wall. If the entire floor has been covered with adhesive, slowly roll the flooring out across the room. Take care to set the flooring firmly into the adhesive as you proceed. When you finish, start at the center of the room and work out any air bubbles that may remain. You can use a rolling pin for this, or rent a floor roller.

Installing flooring with seams. Transfer your floor plan or paper pattern to the flooring as described above. On flooring with a decorative pattern, be sure to leave the margins necessary to match the pattern at the seam on adjoining sheets (see below, left). If your flooring has a simulated grout or mortar joint, plan to cut the seam along the midpoint of the printed joint.

Cut the piece that requires the most intricate fitting first. If you are using adhesive, spread it on the subfloor as directed, stopping 8 or 9 inches from the seam. Then position the sheet on the floor. If you're not using adhesive, simply put the first sheet in place.

Next, cut the second sheet of flooring and position it to overlap the first sheet by at least 2 inches, making sure the design is perfectly aligned. Again, if using adhesive, stop 8 or 9 inches from the seam; if not, position the second sheet carefully, then secure it to the subfloor with two or three strips of double-faced tape.

When the flooring is in position, trim away excess material at each end of the seam in a half-moon shape so the ends butt against the wall.

Using a steel straightedge and a sharp utility knife, make a straight cut—about ½ to ⅝ inch from the edge of the top sheet—down through both sheets of flooring. Lift up the flooring and spread adhesive under the seam. If you're not using adhesive, apply a long piece of double-faced tape beneath the seam. When using an adhesive, clean the area around the seam, using the appropriate solvent for your adhesive. Then use a recommended seam sealer to fuse the two pieces.

Trimming to fit. You'll need to make a series of relief cuts at all inside and outside corners to allow the flooring to lie flat on the floor.

At inside corners, gradually trim away the excess with diagonal cuts until the flooring lies flat (see drawing below). At outside corners, start at the top of the lapped-up flooring and cut straight down to the point where the wall and floor meet.

After you cut the corners, remove the material lapped up against the walls. Using an 18- to 24-inch-long piece of 2 by 4, press the flooring into a right angle where the floor and wall join.

Lay a heavy metal straightedge along the wall and trim the flooring with a utility knife, leaving a gap of about ⅛ inch between the edge of the flooring and the wall. This will allow the material to expand without buckling; the baseboard and/or shoe molding will cover the gap.

RESILIENT TILE FLOORING

Typically, resilient tiles come in 12-inch squares. Other sizes and shapes are available, but they often must be specially ordered for the job.

To determine the amount of tile you need, find the area of the floor, subtracting for any large protrusions such as a peninsula. Add 5 percent so you'll have extra tiles for cutting and later repairs.

HOW TO TRIM RESILIENT TILES

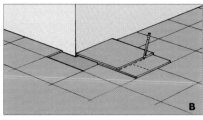

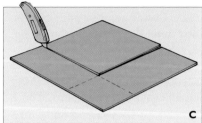

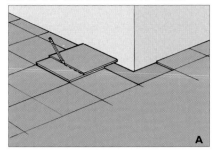

To lay out a border tile, first place a loose tile on top of the last full tile nearest the wall; then place a second tile over the first, butting it against the wall, and mark it for cutting (A). This same technique can be used to mark L-shaped tiles for outside corners (B). Score tiles with a utility knife (C).

If your design uses more than one color or pattern, estimate how many tiles of each kind you'll need by drawing your design on graph paper with colored pencils.

Placing the tiles. Laying resilient tiles involves three steps: marking the working lines, spreading the adhesive (unless you're using self-stick tiles), and placing the tiles. These steps are similar to those for ceramic tile (for details, see pages 100–101). But unlike ceramic tiles, resilient tiles are laid tightly against each other, and, because they're made with machine precision, they must be laid out in perfectly straight lines.

Once a tile is in position, press it firmly in place. Lay half a dozen or so, going over them with a rolling pin. If you're using self-stick tiles, take extra

care to position them exactly before you press them into place (they're hard to remove once they're fixed to the floor). Also note the arrows on the back of self-stick tiles—lay the tiles with the arrows going the same way.

Cutting tile. To cut tiles, score them along the mark with a utility knife; then snap the tile along the line. For intricate cuts, use heavy scissors or tin snips. The tiles will cut more easily if you use a hairdryer to warm them slightly.

To mark border and corner tiles for cutting, position a loose tile exactly over one of the tiles in the last row closest to the wall, making sure that the grain or pattern is running correctly. Place another loose tile on top of the first, butting it against the wall. Using this tile as a guide, mark the tile beneath for cutting, as shown at the top of the page.

HOW TO TRIM FLOORING

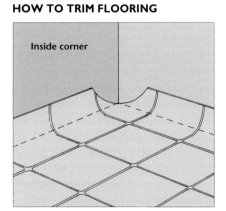

Where flooring turns an inside corner, cut the excess with diagonal cuts.

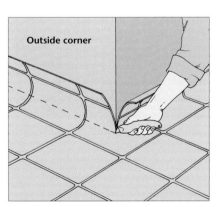

At an outside corner, cut straight down to the point where wall and floor meet.

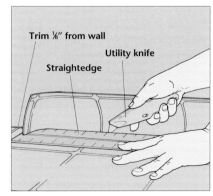

Trim ⅛" from wall
Utility knife
Straightedge

Trim flooring, leaving a ⅛" gap between the edge and the wall.

CERAMIC TILE FLOORS

You can install a ceramic tile floor in a three-step operation: lay evenly spaced tiles in a bed of adhesive atop a smooth, dry, and rigid subfloor; fill the joint spaces between tiles with grout; and seal the floor for durability and easy cleaning. Glazed tiles, thinset adhesive with latex additive, and cement-based grout are probably the best materials for the do-it-yourselfer.

Preparing the subfloor. If at all possible, remove old flooring before installing new ceramic tiles. Not only does this enable you to examine the subfloor and make any necessary repairs, but it should also make the new floor level with floors in adjacent rooms. But if your old resilient (solid, not cushioned) ceramic tile, wood, or masonry flooring is level and in good repair, it can be successfully covered with tile. Your tile dealer can recommend the best adhesive and method of application.

To prepare a plywood subfloor, make certain that all panels are securely attached to the joists. If the subfloor is constructed from individual 4- or 6-inch boards, be sure that each board is securely attached. Drive any protruding nails flush with the surface.

To prevent a board subfloor from warping, or if a plywood subfloor is in poor condition, you'll have to install a new layer over the old one before laying tile. Use exterior or underlayment-grade plywood or particleboard at least $3/8$ inch thick, and leave a $1/16$-inch gap between adjacent panels. Fasten the panels with 6-penny ring-shank nails spaced 6 inches apart. Where possible, drive nails through the panels into the floor joists.

Regardless of your subfloor material, you may need to use a sealer before applying adhesive. Check your adhesive for instructions.

Establish working lines. The key to laying straight rows of tile is to establish proper working lines. You can begin either at the center of the room or at one wall.

If two adjoining walls meet at an exact right angle, start laying tiles along one wall. This method means that fewer border tiles need to be cut; it also allows you to work without stepping on rows previously set.

To check for square corners and straight walls, place a tile tightly into each corner. Stretch a chalkline between the corners of each pair of tiles; pull the line tight and snap each line. Variations in the distance between chalklines and walls will reveal any irregularities in the walls. You can ignore variations as slight as the width of a grout joint. With a carpenter's square, check the intersection of lines in each corner of the room to see if they are square.

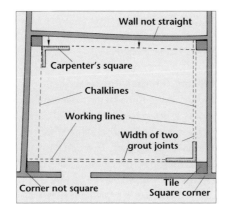

Assuming that your walls are reasonably straight, you can begin laying tile at any straight wall adjoining a straight corner. Snap a new chalkline parallel to the original line and approximately two grout joint widths closer to the center of the room (see drawing above). Lay a similar line, at a right angle to the first, along the adjoining wall. Then nail a batten (wood straightedge) along each of these working lines.

If you can't find a square corner, begin at the center of the room. Locate the center point on each of two opposite walls, and snap a chalkline between the two points. Then find the centers of the other two walls and stretch your chalkline at right angles to the first line; snap the line only after you've used your carpenter's square to determine that the two lines cross at a precise right angle.

Whether you begin at a wall or in the center, it's a good idea to make a dry run before you actually set the tiles in adhesive. Lay the tiles out on the lines, allowing proper spacing for grout joints. Try to determine the best layout while keeping the number of tiles to be cut to a minimum.

Setting the tiles. Using a notched trowel, start spreading a strip of adhesive along one of the battens. Cover about a square yard at first, or the area you can comfortably tile before the adhesive begins to set.

Using a gentle twisting motion, place the first tile in the corner formed by the two battens. With the same motion, place a second tile alongside the first.

To establish the proper width for the grout joint, use molded plastic spacers. Continue laying tiles along the batten until the row is complete. Start each new row at the same end as the first. If you're working from the center of the room, follow one of the patterns shown below.

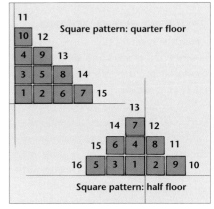

As the tiles are laid, set a piece of carpet-wrapped wood over the tiles; tap it with a mallet or rubber hammer to "beat in" the tiles. Keep checking with a carpenter's square or straightedge to make sure each course is straight. Wiggle any stray tiles back into position while the adhesive is still flexible.

When you're ready to install border tiles, carefully remove the battens. Measure the remaining spaces individually, subtract the width of two grout joints, and mark each tile for any necessary cuts.

HOW TO SET CERAMIC FLOOR TILES

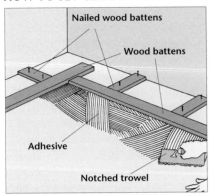

Nail batten boards at right angles, flush with the working lines. Then spread adhesive alongside one batten with a notched trowel.

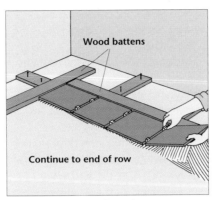

Begin placing tiles from the corner formed by the battens, using spacers to maintain the width of the grout joint. Continue to the end of the first row.

Start each new row at the same end as the first row. To set tiles in adhesive, slide a padded wood beating block over the tiles while tapping it with a hammer.

You can cut tile with a snap cutter (A) rented from your tile supplier or with a power wet saw. To cut irregular shapes, use a tile nipper (B); first score the cutting lines with a glass cutter. Drill holes in the tile with a masonry bit. Smooth any rough edges with an abrasive stone.

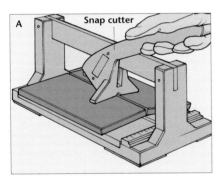

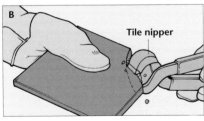

After all the tiles are placed, remove any spacers and clean the tile surface so it's completely free of adhesive. Before applying grout, allow the tiles to set properly—about 24 hours with mastic adhesives.

Applying grout. Grout can be applied liberally around glazed tiles. Grouting unglazed tiles requires more care, since the grout may stain the tile's surface. Be sure to read the manufacturer's recommendations.

Using a rubber-faced float or squeegee, apply grout to the surface of the tile. Force the grout into the joints so they're completely filled; make sure no air pockets remain. Scrape off excess grout with the float, working diagonally across the tiles.

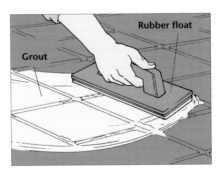

Soak a grouting sponge in clear water and wring it out. Wipe the tiles with a circular motion, removing any remaining grout, until the joints are smooth and level with the tiles. Rinse

and wring out the sponge frequently as you work.

When the tiles are clean, let the grout dry for about 30 minutes. By then, any film of grout left on the tile will have formed a light haze; immediately polish it off with a soft cloth. Smooth grout joints with a jointer, striking tool, or toothbrush handle.

Finishing touches. Most grouts take at least 2 weeks to cure. You'll need to damp cure a cement-based grout by covering the newly installed floor with plastic. Leave the plastic in place for 24 hours; then remove it and allow the grout to cure thoroughly. Stay off the tile until it has cured.

Once the grout has fully cured, seal it and the tile with a silicone or lacquer-based sealer recommended by your tile supplier.

WOOD STRIP FLOORING

Wood strip flooring is the traditional hardwood floor. It is made up of narrow boards or strips with tongue-and-groove edges and ends, laid in random lengths.

You can buy finished or unfinished wood strips. The latter type is more water resistant (joints between boards can be sealed), but prefinished flooring is easier to install.

Though widths and thicknesses vary, the most common strip flooring is $3/4$ inch or $25/32$ inch thick, with a face width of $2\frac{1}{4}$ inches.

Preparing the subfloor. Subfloor preparation can be more demanding than putting in new flooring. Moisture is the number-one enemy of wood floors; you must ensure that the subfloor is completely dry and will remain so. Any crawlspace below the floor must also be properly ventilated and protected from moisture.

Though it's possible to lay wood flooring over an old wood floor that's structurally sound and perfectly level, you may need to remove the old flooring to get down to the subfloor and make necessary repairs or install underlayment. In the long run, this usually provides the most reliable base for your new floor.

Check the exposed subfloor for loose boards or loose plywood panels. If planks are badly bowed and cannot be flattened by nailing, give the floor a rough sanding with a floor sander or cover it with ⅜ or ½-inch plywood or particleboard. Fasten down ⅜-inch material with 3-penny ring-shank or cement-coated nails; for ½-inch material, use 4-penny ring-shank or 5-penny cement-coated nails. Space nails 6 inches apart across the surface of the panels.

New or old, the base for the new floor should be cleaned thoroughly, then covered with a layer of 15-pound asphalt-saturated felt (butting seams) or soft resin paper (overlapping seams 4 inches).

As you put the felt or paper in place, use a straightedge or a chalkline to mark the center of each joist on the covering. The lines will serve as convenient reference points when you attach the new flooring.

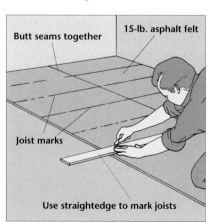

Butt seams together
15-lb. asphalt felt
Joist marks
Use straightedge to mark joists

Planning the new floor. For a trouble-free installation, it is essential that you lay the first course parallel to the center of the kitchen.

Measure the width of the room in several spots and locate the center line as accurately as possible. Snap a chalkline to mark the center. This is your primary reference point.

Next, measuring from the center line, lay out and snap another chalkline about ½ inch from the wall you're using as a starting point.

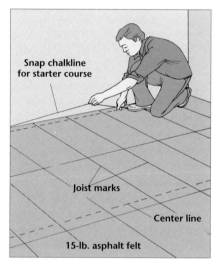

Snap chalkline for starter course

Joist marks

Center line

15-lb. asphalt felt

In a kitchen that's obviously irregular in shape, locate the center line as closely as possible and begin laying the first row of flooring from that point. A special wood strip called a spline is used to join two back-to-back grooved boards along the center line.

Installing the flooring. When starting from the wall, you may need to trim a few boards at the outset. It's important that your first row of flooring line up

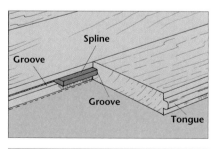

Spline
Groove
Groove
Tongue

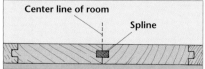

Center line of room
Spline

properly while keeping the ½-inch distance from the wall. If you're starting from the center of an irregular room, the trimming will be done later when you reach the walls.

Tongue-and-groove strip flooring is attached by nailing at an angle through the tongues, where nail heads won't show. (This is called "blind-nailing.") To ensure a tight floor, install strips perpendicular to joists.

You can make a perfectly acceptable installation using basic hand tools, but a nailer (available from most tool rental companies) will speed the work. Similarly, boards can be neatly cut with a backsaw and miter box, but a radial-arm or power miter saw saves time.

If you're starting along the wall, the first row of boards should be secured by face-nailing; the nails will be covered later with shoe molding. Drill pilot holes in the boards slightly smaller than the diameter of your nails.

When beginning at the center of an irregularly shaped room, you can start by blind-nailing through the tongues—with the nailer, if you have one.

Stagger end joints so that no joint is closer than 6 inches to a joint in an adjoining row of boards. Leave approximately ½ inch between each end piece and the wall. As a rule, no end piece should be shorter than 8 inches. When laying flooring over plywood or particleboard, avoid placing the end joints in the flooring directly over joints in the subfloor.

As you place each row, move a block of wood along the leading edge and end of the flooring you've just put down, and give it a sharp rap with a mallet or hammer before you drive each nail. To avoid damaging the tongues, cut a groove in the block, or use a short length of flooring.

Since you won't have enough space to use a nailer until you are several rows from the wall, you'll have to nail the first courses by hand. By continuing to drill holes for the nails, you can keep nails at the proper angle—45° to 50° from the floor—and help prevent splitting. Take care not to crush the upper edges of the boards. Instead of using your hammer to drive nails flush,

HOW TO LAY WOOD-STRIP FLOORING

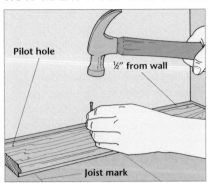

Drill pilot holes slightly smaller than the nail diameter, then face-nail the first course from the wall.

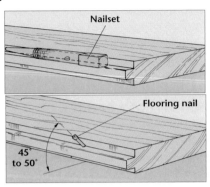

Nail the first few rows by hand—start with a hammer, then drive the nail home with a nailset laid sideways along the tongue.

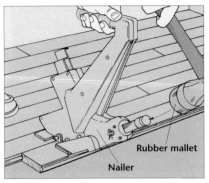

Once there's working room, drive nails with a nailer and rubber mallet; the nailer automatically drives the nails flush.

leave the heads exposed; then place a nailset sideways over each nail along the top of the tongue, and top the nailset with your hammer. Use the nailset's tip to drive the nail flush.

Once you have laid and nailed the first few rows by hand, you can begin to secure the flooring with a nailer, which automatically countersinks all the nails it drives.

When you reach the last few rows, you'll find it difficult to blind-nail the boards. Drill holes and face-nail them. The final strip of flooring must be placed to leave a ½-inch gap between the flooring and the wall. If you're lucky, a standard board will fit. If not, you'll have to rip several boards down to the proper width.

Finishing touches. An unfinished floor has to be sanded and finished. Most equipment rental companies offer the necessary heavy-duty equipment. However, this job is best left to professionals. It involves three sandings, called cuts, using three grades of sandpaper to prepare the floor, then at least two (and preferably three) coats of polyurethane applied with a long-handled mohair-covered paint roller, buffed between each coat with #2 steel wool.

LAMINATE FLOORS

Laminate floors float over a subfloor, expanding or contracting with the temperature and humidity changes of the seasons. Laminate can be installed over existing vinyl, linoleum, or wood floors if the floors are flat and in good condition.

If you are installing laminate over concrete, the concrete must be patched with leveling compound, sanded flat, and covered with a polyethylene vapor barrier that is taped down. On any subfloor, placing a layer of foam or felt on the floor (on top of the vapor barrier with concrete) will help reduce sound.

Install laminate planks so they run parallel to either the longer wall or to the direction of sunlight entering the room with a ¼ inch allowance at the walls for expansion.

To install the boards, start against one wall and build a starter course of three rows, staggering the joints to make them less obvious. Put glue on the tongue or groove of a plank following the manufacturer's directions. Tap on the end of the plank with a tapping block, sliding it into the previous row. Then tap along the long side. Remove excess glue immediately with a

A LOOK AT LAMINATE FLOORS

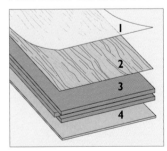

Laminate is composed of four layers: (1) a clear melamine top layer, (2) a design layer made to look like wood or stone, (3) a core of high-density fiberboard, and (4) moisture-resistant backing.

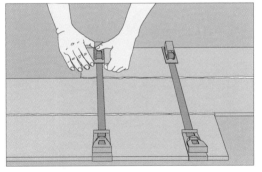

To create a starter course, lay planks in three rows, staggering the joints to make them less obvious. Join with glue and attach special clamps to draw the joints together.

squeegee to prevent a haze from forming at the seams, and wipe the board clean with a cloth. Attach special clamps or straps, available from the manufacturer, to draw the joints together. Make sure the first course is straight by making a chalkline on the floor or by using the pattern of the existing floor as a guide. Allow this first course to set for the time specified by the manufacturer.

Continue to lay planks to complete a row. Insert spacers (either pieces of wood or plastic spacers provided by the manufacturer) at the ends next to the walls before moving to the next row. Reset the clamps as each row is added, applying enough pressure to make a good bond. Wedge the last row into place using a scrap of wood and a chisel or bar.

After the glue has set, remove the spacers and attach base molding. Allow the floor to set for at least 12 to 24 hours before moving furniture onto it.

Disk faucets, double self-rimmed sinks, built-in dishwashers, microwave ovens—the array of styles, colors, and special features available in kitchen fixtures and appliances can be bewildering. For help in making your selection, see pages 54–63.

Fortunately for the do-it-yourselfer, most variations of the basic fixtures and appliances are installed in a similar manner. The following pages cover the fundamentals. Specific instructions should accompany each unit (check before you make a purchase); follow the manufacturer's instructions if they differ from those below.

Many fixtures and appliances can be easily connected to an existing sink drain or electrical outlet. But before you make any purchase, be sure your home's plumbing and electrical systems can handle the new load. Check your local codes. For a discussion of plumbing and electrical systems, their limitations, and applicable codes, see "Plumbing basics," pages 74–76, and "Electrical basics," pages 77–82.

Sometimes the greatest challenge of replacing a major appliance such as a refrigerator is transporting the old one from the site and bringing in the new one. Always plan your route in advance ("Do we need to remove a door? How will we get it down the steps?"), and have adequate help on hand. An appliance dolly can be indispensable.

INSTALLING A FAUCET

Most modern kitchen faucets are the deck-mounted type, seated on the rear of the sink and secured from below. When shopping for a replacement, you'll find the selection staggering. You can choose from a lineup of single-lever washerless faucets—valve, disk, ball, and cartridge—and styles ranging from antique reproductions to futuristic compression models. All are interchangeable as long as the new faucet's inlet shanks are spaced to fit the holes on the sink.

If you still have old-fashioned wall-mounted faucets, you face a different decision: either buy a new model, of which there are many styles, or switch to a deck-mounted type. If you decide to use a different type of faucet, you'll be adding several steps to the installation process; at the very minimum, you'll need to reroute pipes from the wall into the base cabinet and patch the wall.

Removing a deck-mounted faucet.

Begin by shutting off the water supply, either at the shutoff valves on both hot and cold water supply lines or (if you don't have shutoff valves) at the main house shutoff near the water meter.

Then drain the pipes by opening the faucet or faucets.

Use a wrench to unfasten the couplings that attach the supply tubing to the shutoff valves. If space is cramped under the sink, use a basin wrench to loosen and remove the locknuts and washers on both faucet inlet shanks.

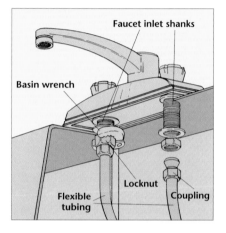

On a kitchen sink equipped with a spray hose attachment, undo the locknuts connecting the hose to the faucet body and the hose nipple. Then lift the faucet away from the sink.

Installing the new faucet. Clean the surface of the sink where the new faucet will sit. Some faucets come with a rubber gasket on the bottom; if yours doesn't, apply a bead of plumber's putty or silicone to the base.

To set the faucet in position, you

HOW TO INSTALL FAUCETS

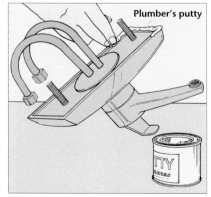

Apply plumber's putty to the bottom edge of the faucet body if there's no gasket to seal it to the sink's surface.

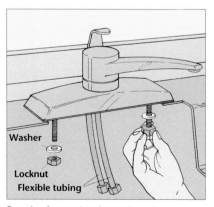

Set the faucet in place, threading supply tubes through the sink hole; then tighten the locknuts.

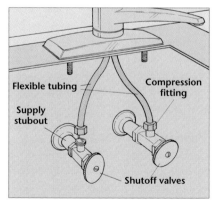

Attach flexible tubing to the shutoff valves, using appropriate compression fittings.

need to simultaneously feed the flexible supply tubing, if attached, down through the middle sink hole. (If your new faucet has no tubing included, buy two lengths of tubing and attach them at this point.) Press the faucet onto the sink's surface. Install any required washers and locknuts from below; tighten them with a wrench. Attach a spray hose according to the manufacturer's instructions.

Run the flexible tubing to the shut-off valves, gently bending the tubing as necessary with a plumber's bending tool. Connect it using compression fittings. (If you don't have shutoff valves and would like to install them in your system, consult a plumber.)

INSTALLING A SINK

A deck-mounted kitchen sink fits into a specially cut hole in the countertop. If you're simply replacing a sink, you can choose any model the same size as the present sink or larger; if it's a new installation, you'll have to make the sink cutout first.

SINK DRAIN ELEMENTS

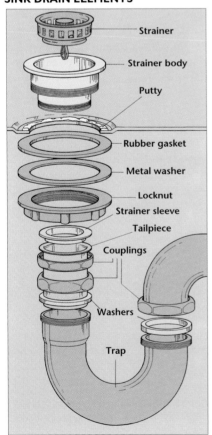

- Strainer
- Strainer body
- Putty
- Rubber gasket
- Metal washer
- Locknut
- Strainer sleeve
- Tailpiece
- Couplings
- Washers
- Trap

Three basic sink types prevail: self-rimmed, rimmed, and recessed, or undermounted. Most new sinks are self-rimmed; these have a molded overlap that's supported by the edge of the countertop cutout. A rimmed sink has metal strips that hold the sink to the countertop. An undermounted sink is held in place beneath the countertop by metal clips.

A fourth type, the integral sink, is part of the countertop and is available with either solid-surface or stainless steel countertops.

Removing an old sink. First shut off the water supply at the shutoff valves on both hot and cold water supply pipes; if you don't have shutoff valves, turn off the water at the main house shutoff. Then drain the pipes by opening the faucet, and disconnect the supply pipes as described on page 104. You'll also need to disconnect the drain trap from the sink's strainer assembly. Loosen the couplings that hold the tailpiece to the strainer assembly and the tailpiece to the trap. Push the tailpiece down into the trap.

From below the sink, remove any clamps or lugs holding it to the countertop. If necessary, break the putty seal by forcing the sink free.

Making a sink cutout. For a new installation, trace either a template (included with the new sink) or the bottom edge of the frame onto the exact spot where the sink will sit. Generally, 1½ to 2 inches is left between the edge of the cutout and the front edge of the countertop. Drill pilot holes in each corner of the outline, and insert a saber saw into one of the holes to make the cutout.

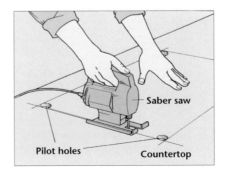

- Saber saw
- Pilot holes
- Countertop

Installing the new sink. It's best to mount the faucet and hook up the strainer assembly before installing the new sink in the countertop.

To install a strainer assembly, first apply a bead of plumber's putty to the underlip of the strainer body, then press it down into the sink opening. If the strainer is held in place by a locknut, place the rubber gasket and metal washer over the strainer body and tighten by hand. Hold the strainer from above while you snug up the locknut, preferably with a spud wrench. If the strainer is held in place by a retainer, fit the retainer over the strainer body and tighten all three screws. Attach the tailpiece with a coupling.

Some self-rimmed sinks include a rubber gasket below the lip. In any case, apply a ½-inch-wide strip of putty or silicone caulk along the edge of the countertop opening. Set the sink into the cutout, pressing it down. Smooth out any excess putty.

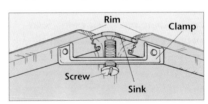

- Rim
- Clamp
- Screw
- Sink

For a rimmed sink, apply a ring of plumber's putty around the top edge of the sink. Fasten the frame to the sink, following the manufacturer's instructions; some frames attach with metal corner clamps, others with metal extension tabs that bend around the sink lip. Wipe off any excess putty.

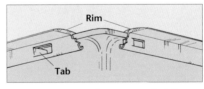

- Rim
- Tab

Anchor an undermounted sink from below at 6- or 8-inch intervals, using any clamps or lugs provided. You may also need to drill separate holes in the countertop for the faucet or accessory fittings.

Finally, hook up the supply pipes and drain trap. Turn on the water and check for leaks.

INSTALLING A GARBAGE DISPOSER

Installing a disposer takes a few hours, but the basic connection is not difficult. Most units fit the standard 3½ or 4-inch drain outlets of kitchen sinks and mount somewhat like a sink strainer (see page 105).

Plumbing a disposer involves altering the sink trap to fit the unit. If your model has direct wiring, you must run electrical cable to a nearby junction box or other power source (see pages 77–82 for information). Plug-in disposers require a 120-volt grounded (three-prong) outlet under the sink and a separate wall switch adjacent to the sink.

Before installing a disposer, check plumbing codes for any restrictions.

Removing a strainer or disposer. If you're adding a disposer for the first time, first disconnect the sink strainer assembly. Start by removing the tailpiece and trap (see page 105); then disassemble the strainer components and lift them out of the sink. Clean away any old putty or sealing gaskets around the opening.

If you're replacing a disposer, first turn off the electricity; then unplug the unit or disconnect the wiring. Loosen the screws on the mounting ring

assembly and remove the parts; finally, remove the sink flange by lifting it from above.

Mounting the disposer. The disposer comes with its own sink flange and mounting assembly. Run a bead of plumber's putty around the sink opening and seat the flange. Then, working from below, slip the gasket, mounting rings, and snap ring up onto the neck of the flange. The snap ring should fit firmly into a groove on the sink flange to hold things in place temporarily.

Uniformly tighten the slotted screws in the mounting rings until the gasket fits snugly against the bottom of the flange. Remove any excess putty around the flange.

Attach the drain elbow to the disposer. Lift the disposer into place, aligning the holes in the dispenser's flange with the slotted screws in the mounting rings. Rotate the disposer so that the drain elbow lines up with the drainpipe. Tighten the nuts securely onto the slotted screws to ensure a good seal.

Making the hookups. Fit the coupling and washer onto the drain elbow. Add an elbow fitting on the other end of the trap to adjust to the drainpipe. You

may need to shorten the drainpipe to make the connection. Tighten all the connections, and run water through the disposer to check for leaks.

At this point, either plug the disposer into a grounded outlet (see pages 80–81), or shut off the power and wire the unit directly, following the manufacturer's instructions. Then turn the power back on. To be completely safe, it's important to test the unit to make sure it has been properly grounded.

INSTALLING A DISHWASHER

A built-in dishwasher requires three connections: hot water supply, drainpipe fitting, and a 120-volt, 20-amp, grounded plug-in outlet. (For basic electrical information, see pages 77–82.)

Local codes may require that you also install a venting device, called an air gap, on the sink or countertop. Some areas require a permit and an inspection when a built-in dishwasher is installed; check your local plumbing codes before you begin the work.

Making new connections. For a first-time installation, you'll need to tap into the hot water supply pipe under the sink, and into either the garbage disposer or sink drainpipe to ensure the proper drainage.

HOW TO PLUMB A GARBAGE DISPOSER

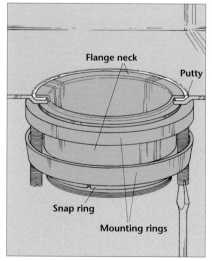

Attach mounting rings, with a gasket and snap ring, to the sink flange; tighten the slotted screws.

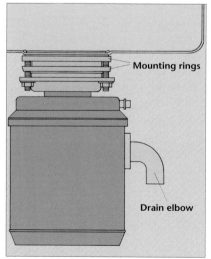

Line up the drain elbow on the disposer so it's directly opposite the drainpipe; tighten nuts onto the slotted screws.

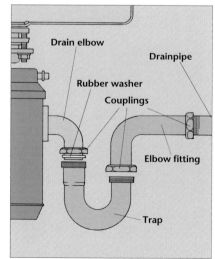

Connect the trap to the disposer's drain elbow and to the elbow fitting on the drainpipe.

Begin by shutting off the water supply, either at the shutoff valves under the sink or at the main house shutoff. Drain the supply pipes by turning on the sink faucets. Cut into the hot water supply pipe and install a tee fitting. (If you need any help with pipefitting techniques, consult a professional plumber.) Run flexible copper or plastic tubing (depending on your model) to the location of the water inlet valve on the dishwasher. To simplify future repairs, install a shutoff valve.

Your dishwasher can drain either into the sink drain above the trap or into a garbage disposer. For use with a sink drain, you'll need to buy a threaded waste tee fitting (see the center drawing below).

To install a waste tee, remove the sink tailpiece (see page 105) and insert the waste tee into the trap. Cut the tailpiece so it fits between the waste tee and the sink strainer assembly. Reattach the tailpiece and clamp the dishwasher drain hose onto the waste tee fitting.

If you already have (or are now installing) a garbage disposer, plan to attach the dishwasher drain hose to the disposer drain fitting on the disposer's side. First turn off the electrical circuit that controls the disposer. Then use a screwdriver to punch out the knockout plug inside the fitting. Clamp the dishwasher drain hose to the fitting.

To prevent a backup of waste water into the dishwasher, make a gradual loop with the drain hose to the height of the dishwasher's top before making the connection. If you're required to install an air gap instead of the loop, insert the air gap into the already drilled hole found on some sinks, or into a hole you've drilled at the back of the countertop. Screw the air gap tight from below.

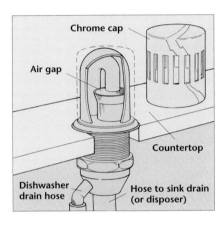

Run one length of hose from the dishwasher to the air gap, and another from the air gap to the waste tee or disposer.

Removing an old dishwasher. If you're simply replacing a dishwasher, the connections should already be made. But you'll have to disconnect and remove the old unit before installing the new one.

First, unfasten any screws or brackets anchoring the dishwasher to the countertop or the floor. Turn off the electrical power to the circuit controlling the dishwasher; then shut off the water supply. Disconnect the supply hookup and the drain hose from the dishwasher. With a helper, pull the unit forward to gain access to the electrical connection (unless it's under the sink). If the dishwasher is the plug-in type, you're in luck. If it was wired directly, disconnect the wires from the dishwasher.

Completing the installation. Plug in the new dishwasher or reconnect the hookup wires, then slide it into place. Complete the supply and drain hookups according to the manufacturer's instructions.

Level the dishwasher by adjusting the height of the legs. Anchor the unit to the underside of the countertop with any screws provided. Consider facing the refrigerator to match surrounding cabinetry; panels are available with most modular cabinet lines.

HOW TO CONNECT A DISHWASHER

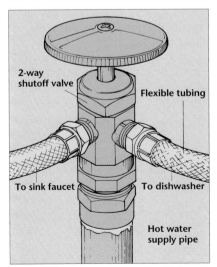

Install a two-way valve or a tee fitting and shutoff valve in the hot water supply pipe, then add flexible tubing.

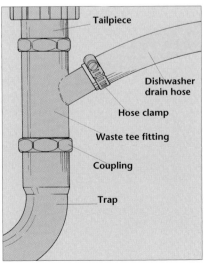

To drain into a sink trap, add a threaded waste tee fitting between tailpiece and trap.

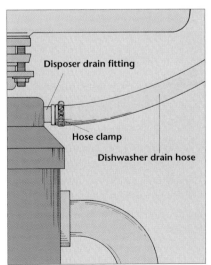

To drain into a garbage disposer, connect a dishwasher drain hose to the disposer's drain fitting.

INSTALLING A HOT WATER DISPENSER

Easy-to-install hot water dispensers incorporate a stainless steel faucet connected to an undercounter storage tank. The tank, which in turn is connected to a nearby cold water pipe, has an electric heating coil that keeps water at about 200°F—50° hotter than that produced by the average water heater. NOTE: A hot water dispenser should not be installed where small children can reach it.

Most units plug into a 120-volt grounded outlet installed under the sink. (For electrical details, see pages 77–82.) Some models, though, are directly wired to a grounded junction box.

Positioning the dispenser. Begin by deciding where you want to place the unit. Commonly, the faucet fits in a hole at the rear of the sink rim, or else mounts directly on the countertop. In the latter case, cut a 1¼-inch-diameter hole in your countertop near the sink rim with an electric drill fitted with a hole saw or spade bit. Follow the manufacturer's instructions to attach the dispenser faucet from beneath the sink. Generally, you'll need only to install a nut and washers to hold the faucet.

From inside the sink cabinet, screw the tank mounting bracket to the wall or cabinet back, making sure it's plumb. The bracket should be located about 14 inches below the underside of the countertop. Next, mount the tank on the bracket.

Making the connections. Before plumbing the unit, shut off the water supply and drain the pipes by opening the sink faucets. Many dispensers come with a self-tapping valve. If yours doesn't, tap into the cold water pipe using a saddle tee fitting (see the drawing below). To tap into the cold water pipe, clamp the fitting to the supply pipe and drill a hole through the fitting into the pipe.

If saddle tees aren't permitted in your area, tap in with a standard tee fitting, then install a shutoff valve and reducer fitting for the dispenser's water supply tube. (If you need help, consult a professional plumber.)

Using the compression nuts provided with the unit, attach one water supply tube between the dispenser and the storage tank, and another between the tank and the cold water supply pipe. Turn on the water supply and check for leaks. Plug in the unit—or shut off the power and connect the wires directly, as required.

INSTALLING A REFRIGERATOR

Installing a new refrigerator is easy work—just plug it into a 120-volt, 20-amp appliance circuit. Your only real challenge will be handling and transporting both the old and the new refrigerators.

To help make it easier to move these heavy appliances, work with a partner and use pieces of old carpeting or rugs, or large pieces of corrugated cardboard. Have one person tilt the refrigerator backward slightly so the other person can slip the carpet pieces or cardboard under the front legs. Then tilt the refrigerator frontward slightly while slipping carpet pieces under the back legs. Now you can slide the refrigerator out without damaging the kitchen floor.

Disconnecting a refrigerator. When removing an old refrigerator, simply pull it out any way you can to gain access to the plug. If the unit has an automatic icemaker, the fitting attaching the copper supply tubing must be disconnected. Be prepared to remove doors from their hinges, guard rails from stairways, or any other obstructions in the path. Then secure the refrigerator to an appliance dolly and wheel it out.

HOW TO HOOK UP A HOT WATER DISPENSER

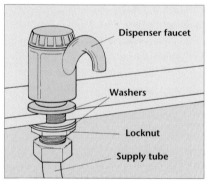

First, secure the dispenser faucet to the sink rim or countertop from below, using a locknut and washers.

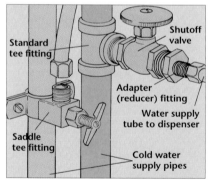

Tap into the cold water supply pipe with a saddle tee or standard tee fitting and shutoff valve.

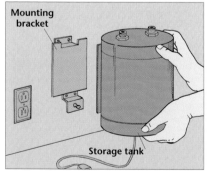

Attach the tank mounting bracket to the wall or cabinet back, then install the storage tank.

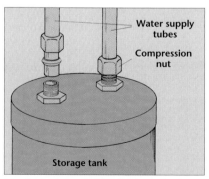

Hook up one supply tube from the dispenser to the storage tank, and one from the tank to the supply pipe.

For safety's sake, store the old refrigerator with its door or doors removed.

Positioning a new refrigerator.
Wheel the replacement into a position where you can hook up the icemaker, if necessary, and plug the refrigerator in. Finally, push it into place and check level. Adjust the level with shims, as necessary.

A refrigerator can be given a built-in look—just wrap modular cabinets around it, or install custom-made cabinets. Be sure to allow ½ inch to 1 inch on all sides for easy removal and air circulation. Add a decorative face panel or manufacturer's trim kit as required.

Installing a water line.
A water dispenser or icemaker is connected by ¼-inch copper tubing to a cold water supply pipe. To make the connection, use a saddle tee or standard tee fitting and shutoff valve, as detailed under "Installing a hot water dispenser," on page 108. If the refrigerator can be easily reached from the sink complex, tap in there through the sides of the base cabinets. If the refrigerator is far from the sink, look for another cold water supply pipe to tap (see "Plumbing basics," pages 74–76, for help).

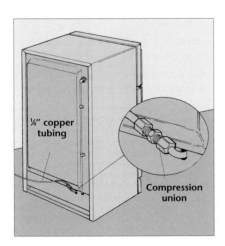

¼" copper tubing

Compression union

At the refrigerator end, leave a few extra loops of tubing to help you position the unit. Attach the tubing to the refrigerator with a compression union (see drawing above) or other special fitting, following the manufacturer's instructions.

INSTALLING COOKTOPS, RANGES, AND WALL OVENS
Cooking equipment offers you a choice of two energy sources—electricity or gas. In addition, it offers three designs—a freestanding or "slide-in" range, a drop-in range, or a combination of a built-in cooktop and separate wall ovens. For a detailed breakdown and evaluation of your options, see pages 58–60.

The only factors limiting your choice are the capacity of your present gas or electrical system, the distance from an existing connection that you plan to move new equipment, and the labor and expense of switching from electricity to gas or vice versa.

To analyze your present electrical system, see pages 77–78. An electric range, wall oven, or cooktop must be powered by an individual 240-volt circuit. (The exception is a microwave oven, which requires only 120-volt current.) Some appliances are direct wired; others plug into special 30-, 40-, or 50-amp outlets mounted nearby. Plugs and outlets are not interchangeable. To determine your needs, consult your appliance dealer or a licensed electrician.

For a discussion of gas system basics, see page 76. If you plan to use the existing line, a gas range can usually be relocated as far as 6 feet from the old gas connection. For new gas lines, you should hire a licensed plumber unless you're very well versed in gas installations. Check your local codes to see if you are permitted to install a gas line yourself. In any case, the work will require inspection by your building department or utility company before the gas can be turned on.

Once your electrical or gas lines are in proper order, the actual hookup is quite straightforward.

Removing a range, oven, or cooktop.
Before removing the old unit, first determine the method by which it is fastened (if it is fastened); for help, refer to the appropriate section on page 110.

You'll probably need to unfasten some screws or clamps attaching the unit to the underside of the countertop or to adjacent cabinets.

After removing the fasteners, move the appliance just far enough to gain access to the electrical or gas connection. If the appliance is electric, shut off the circuit to the appliance or appliance group before beginning the removal.

Gas appliances should have individual shutoff valves (see drawing below). The valve is open when the handle is parallel to the pipe; to shut off the gas supply, turn the handle until it forms a right angle with the pipe. The appliance is connected to the shutoff valve and main gas line with either solid pipe or flexible tubing and compression fittings.

Solid pipe will need to be cut or unthreaded. A flexible connector can be removed from the shutoff valve with an adjustable wrench.

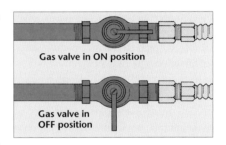

Gas valve in ON position

Gas valve in OFF position

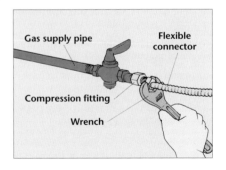

Gas supply pipe

Flexible connector

Compression fitting

Wrench

Some gas appliances also have a 120-volt electrical connection that powers lights, timers, or a thermostat. Unplug it or, if the connection is wired directly, shut off power to the circuit before disconnecting the wires.

If at any point you're unsure about how to proceed, call your utility company or seek other knowledgeable help.

Once both the fasteners and power connection are disassembled, the unit can be freely lifted or pulled out of position, loaded onto an appliance dolly, and transported from the room. Be sure you have adequate help for heavy jobs.

Installing a freestanding range.

Except for the bulkiness of these units, this is a simple job to perform. Be sure the gas shutoff valve or electrical outlet is already in place. Slide the unit in partway until you can make the power hookup; then position it exactly. If the range has adjustable legs, raise or lower them to level the unit; otherwise, use shims as necessary.

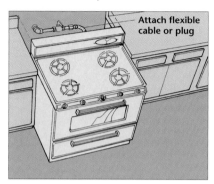

Attach flexible cable or plug

If you plan to use an existing gas connection, the new range must be within 6 feet of the shutoff valve. Check local gas or plumbing codes to determine if a hook-up is a do-it-yourself job or requires a professional and to see if the connector may be flexible copper, brass, or aluminum or if it must be solid pipe. A flexible connector is much simpler to install. Use an adjustable wrench to attach the connector's compression nuts to both range and shutoff as required.

Before turning the gas supply back on, it's wise to have utility company personnel check your work. They can inspect for gas leaks or air in the line, and can light and adjust the pilot lights on your new range.

Installing a drop-in range.

This type of range is lowered into place between adjacent base cabinets. You'll need to determine the best method for attaching the power connection (either electric plug or gas connector) before, during, or after lifting the unit into the correct position.

Some units have self-supporting flanges that sit on adjacent countertop surfaces. Others are simply lowered into place atop a special cabinet base. Fasten these ranges through side slots into the adjacent cabinets, or into the base itself. Bases and front trim that match the surrounding cabinetry are available with many cabinet lines, or you can have them custom-made.

Flange supports range

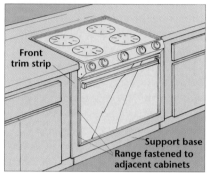

Front trim strip

Support base
Range fastened to adjacent cabinets

Installing a cooktop.

Standard gas and electric cooktops or combination cooktop-barbecue units are dropped into a countertop cutout, much as a new sink is installed (see page 105). They are then anchored from below with hardware supplied by the manufacturer. The power connection is in the cabinet directly below or to one side of the unit.

Electric cooktops may be plugged in or directly wired to a nearby junction box. A gas cooktop is normally connected by a flexible connector

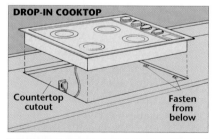

DROP-IN COOKTOP

Countertop cutout

Fasten from below

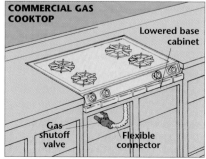

COMMERCIAL GAS COOKTOP

Lowered base cabinet

Gas shutoff valve

Flexible connector

(check local codes) and must be located within 3 feet of its shutoff valve.

Commercial gas cooktops sit on their own legs on the countertop. Often, a lowered base cabinet is used to align the cooktop with the surrounding countertop. Because of its resistance to heat, tile is frequently used below the cooktop; steel strips help shield adjacent cabinets. The flexible gas connector is commonly run through a hole drilled into the base cabinet below.

Many cooktops, especially those in islands or peninsulas, have special down-venting components that direct smoke, grease, and moisture to a fan located in the base cabinet below. From that point, ducting runs out through the wall or down through the cabinet base and below the floor, as shown on page 111.

Installing a wall oven.

Separate wall ovens, either singly or in pairs, are housed in specially designed wall cabinets available in many sizes. Choose your wall oven first, and take the specifications with you when you shop for cabinets.

Wall ovens typically slide into place and rest atop support shelves. They're fastened to the cabinet through the sides or through overlapping flanges on the front. Trim strips are commonly available to fill any gaps between the ovens and the cabinet front.

The plug-in outlet or gas shutoff valve is usually located below the oven or ovens, inside the cabinet. If you plan both a microwave and a standard electric oven, you'll need both 120-volt and 120/240-volt outlets.

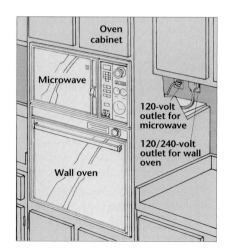

Oven cabinet

Microwave

120-volt outlet for microwave

120/240-volt outlet for wall oven

Wall oven

INSTALLING A VENTILATION HOOD

The two basic types of ventilation hoods are ducted and ductless. Though the ductless type is far easier to install (it requires no ductwork), the ducted version is far more efficient.

Before planning any ducting or purchasing materials, check local mechanical codes for requirements.

Ducting basics. If you're simply replacing a ducted vent hood with a new one, you can probably use the old ducting to vent the new hood.

If you're starting from scratch, keep in mind that the straighter and shorter the path is from the hood to the outside, the more efficient the hood will be. Ducting can run either vertically through the roof or out through the wall.

Ducting is available in both metal and plastic, and is either rectangular or round. The round type is available in both rigid and flexible varieties. The flexible type, though not as strong as the rigid sort, will follow a more twisted course without requiring fittings at each bend. However, if you use round ducting of either type, you'll have to provide a transition fitting where the ducting meets the vent hood.

Join sections of ducting with aluminum tape, not duct tape. If any elbow fittings are required, you'll need access to make the connection. Outside,

HOW TO MOUNT A VENT HOOD

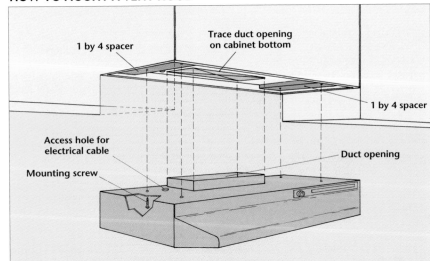

To mount a vent hood, trace the duct opening and electrical cable knockout hole on the wall cabinet or wall. Make the cutout with a drill and saber saw. If the cabinet bottom is recessed, add spacers to provide flush mounting surfaces.

protect the opening with either a flanged wall cap or a roof cap with integral flashing. Caulk around a wall cap to seal the seams between flange and siding. A roof cap's flashing must first be slipped under the roofing material; then all seams are liberally covered with roofing cement.

Mounting the hood. A vent hood is most commonly mounted on the bottom of a wall cabinet. But first you must cut holes in the cabinet to match knockout holes on the vent's shell: one hole for the duct connector

and one hole for the electrical cable.

The hood is screwed to the bottom of the cabinet. If the bottom is recessed, you'll have to add spacers to attach the unit, as shown above.

Follow the manufacturer's instructions to hook up the electrical wires, making sure to attach the grounding screw to the grounding bracket on the hood.

Using sheet metal screws, connect the vent hood's duct connector to the ducting inside the cabinet. Finally, install light bulbs, the lighting panel, and the filter panel.

THREE PATHS FOR A VENT DUCT

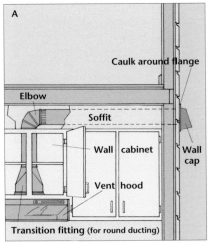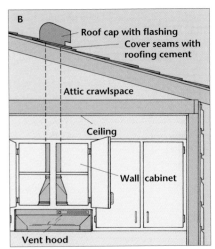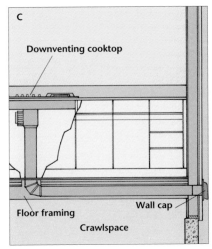

To route ducting from a vent hood, run it horizontally in the space between wall cabinets and ceiling or behind a soffit (A); or take the direct route up through the cabinet and ceiling to the roof (B). A downventing unit vents a cooktop in an island or peninsula (C).